Discover the **'fastest way to slow down'**

cool canals
slow getaways and different days

THE GUIDE

Phillippa Greenwood and Martine O'Callaghan

ISBN 978-09560699-00

Published March 2009 by
Coolcanals Guides
128 Newtown Road
Malvern, Worcestershire, WR14 1PF
info@coolcanalsguides.com
www.coolcanalsguides.com

OUR THANKS

to everyone who helped in the making of
this guidebook, especially: Ann O'Callaghan,
Mollie Lloyd, Teresa Atkins, George Lloyd,
all the people on the waterways appearing
in photographs inside this guidebook and
our stalwart companions - the cats.

Thanks also to those who have absolutely
nothing to do with this guidebook, but help
to make the world a better place: WSPA,
RSPCA, CIWF, Brooke Foundation,
Woodland Trust, Amnesty International.

OUR ETHICS & THE ENVIRONMENT

We want to inspire visitors to keep using
their waterways and help Britain's canals
stay alive. At the same time, we never
knowingly support any business or activity
not in keeping with the community, culture
and traditions that make our canals special.

Because we care about the whole earth as
well as the waterways, we 'think' green
throughout every part of the process of
making our guides: from using Ecotricity in
our office and never driving if we can walk
to choosing eco award-winning UK printers.

Printed and bound in the UK by
Butler Tanner & Dennis, Frome, Somerset

Cool Canals is printed using 100% vegetable-based
inks on Condat Silk FSC paper, produced from
100% Elemental Chlorine Free (EFC) pulp that is
fully recyclable. It has a Forest Stewardship
Council (FSC) certification and is fully manufactured
on one site by Condat in France, an ISO14001
accredited company. All FSC certified papers are
produced by companies who support well-managed
forestry schemes which in turn actively plant and
replace trees that are cut down for pulp, typically
planting more trees than are harvested. Butler
Tanner and Dennis are also fully ISO14001 accredited
and, by both printing and binding on one site,
dramatically reduce their impact on the environment.

Contents

The special thing about canals

Everyone needs an antidote to the mayhem of modern living, so why not do something different? Eat strawberries on a boat, run through a tunnel, canoe over an aqueduct or stroll a slow mile.

The minute you arrive, you sense canals are different to any place you've been before. There's water, boats, heritage and charismatic landscapes, then there's the discovery of endless activities and adventures - yet it's the simplicity of camaraderie with an 'anything goes' culture that makes this destination special. Whether you're hippy or grunge, urban or floral, Imelda Marcos or barefoot, when you step into the world of canals, you can do what you want, wear what you want, be who you are. The only enforced rule is to willingly immerse yourself in the slow culture. Perhaps their egalitarianism comes from canals historically defying every social and geographical boundary in their way. Travel defines this place, making friendships immediate and transient. Free from the clutter of materialism and the stress of the rush hour, people become nonchalant to differences that might mean more in the outside world.

Canals don't make trendy overstatements or jump on image-conscious bandwagons. So whether you're ludicrously old or still only small, rich, poor, fit or not, and if you want to sip city cocktails, take the kids out on a boat, run with your dog or dance with the ducks - so long as you nod as you pass by, it's cool. The mix of water with the great outdoors makes anyone feel welcome, but don't worry about crowds spoiling your fun - mass tourism is too busy hurtling elsewhere on motorways to notice the parallel world of canals where nothing moves faster than 4mph.

No frills, no fuss, this is seriously slow Britain.

Introduction to this guidebook

The inland waterways have become the nation's new leisure destination, with its own prosaic claim to be 'the fastest way to slow down'. The waterways world is seeing a boom in visitors - not that you'd guess. With over 2,000 miles of water road, it's easy to escape the crowds and relax in rural solitude. It's the car-free slow destination waiting to be explored: a place to chill out, do something different, somewhere to escape the mayhem and focus. Ignore the credit crunch: if you want to lash out on expensive overblown waterways holidays, you can – but there's plenty to enjoy that's absolutely free too.

In this guide we share some of the best places we've found and great ways to enjoy special time on Britain's inland waterways. The possibilities are endless! 'Cool canals' aims to inspire and inform so that you can explore the waterways world in your own way, whether that's paddling your own canoe, sightseeing, or letting your hair down at a waterside festival. We don't give nitty-gritty history or navigation details of each canal, there are plenty of other books that do that. 'Cool canals' is all about how to spend leisure time on the waterside, and water. What we've liked along our travels we want to tell you about, but we can't fit everything into this guide, so we try to offer the best flavour of what's out there.

Our philosophy is simple. We love the freedom of the great waterways outdoors with the peace and unhurried pace so rare to find. Our pursuit is slow adventure, unpretentious comforts, slow eating and drinking, discovering new places and cultures. Sometimes it's about getting away from it all in the middle of nowhere, and sometimes it's fun to go sightseeing or mingle with the locals.

Let this book guide you, then discover your own way.

Introduction to canals

While tides crash onto coastal rocks, and rivers flow from the hills, gentler waters hold the secret tranquillity of inland Britain. People don't come here to conquer, or just stand in awe; they participate, slowing themselves from the pace of modern living.

Roving from the wild Highlands of Scotland to the sands of Cornwall, canals touch the Pennines, the Dales, the Peak District, Brecon Beacons, Birmingham, Stratford-upon-Avon, Bath and almost everywhere between.

Don't be fooled by the idyllic tranquillity. Canals are extreme destinations, with high aqueducts and tumbling lock flights linking urban chic to real countryside. Rambling water roads whisper from the past to attract visitors today and, for a lucky few, the waterways are even home. So what are the secrets of these powerful, modest waters?

The blunt reality is that today's peaceful linear landscape, so alive with wildlife and nature, was built over 200 years ago by the slavery of navvies for the profits of industrialisation. Great engineers such as Brindley and Telford created essential transport routes for entrepreneurs including Salt, Cadbury and Wedgwood in an era when the booming British manufacturing industry was dominating world economics. Raw materials and products, coal, pottery, lace, iron and salt, were carried by horse-drawn narrowboats along the motorways of the time.

Canals stood for the status of material power and the new urbanism. Created for speed, canals now ironically offer space in which to slow down and escape from the very urban success they helped build. History probably wouldn't mind the twist of fate.

Where man-made canals blend into countryside, a unique landscape evolves. The true colours of the canal have always been brightly painted narrowboats and added charm comes with the oddly romantic black and white paint used uniformly to protect lock arms, signposts and mooring dollies.

The waterways can boast tunnels blasting through mountains and bridges flying over rivers, yet the simple workings of canal locks fascinate. Basic awesome physics and the mechanics of chunky oiled cogs make still water travel up and down hills in the same way centuries after the canals were built. Lifting tons of water and steel narrowboats with the turn of even a frail hand will always defy logic.

In Britain, half of us live within five miles of a waterway (often without realising) and those who wander onto the quiet towpaths enter a different world. Antidotes to stress come with the clinking of mooring rings, the hoot of an invisible moorhen, the occasional splosh of a bathing duck and the chilled put-put of approaching narrowboats. Whether you holiday in a boat or just take a stroll along a towpath, it's impossible not to be drawn into the spirit of the waterways.

Nowhere in Britain is quite like the canals.

UK canal map & Regional finder

Scotland
Pages 29, 36, 37, 54, 57, 65, 76, 91, 96, 101, 117, 123, 130, 141, 146, 165, 170, 173, 178, 181, 186, 189, 239, 243

Wales
Pages 26, 29, 35-38, 45, 51, 64, 79, 85, 91, 101, 130, 141, 162, 165, 173, 177, 181, 189, 201-207, 239, 243

North
Pages 24, 29, 36, 38, 45, 52, 57, 73, 76, 79, 88, 91, 95 ,96, 101, 111, 117-119, 123, 130, 153, 165, 173, 181, 186, 189, 219-225, 239, 240, 243

South
Pages 26, 29, 35-37, 41, 45, 57, 63, 74-76, 79, 85, 87, 88, 91, 97, 98, 101, 109, 111, 117, 123, 129, 130, 146, 157, 161, 162, 165, 170, 173, 177, 181, 189, 209-215, 240, 243

Heart of England
Pages 25, 29, 36, 41, 45, 53, 57, 73, 79, 86, 87, 91, 101, 106, 107, 123, 130, 141, 157, 161, 165, 170, 173, 178, 181, 185, 189, 193-199, 227-233, 240

Waterways highlights
The 7 Wonders of the Waterways: Pages 37, 38, 63, 64, 87, 95, 203, 239, 240, 243
Waterways Museums: Pages 109, 111, 129, 245

If you're looking for something specific
Throughout this guidebook, we've tried to be inclusive but can only mention disabled access, star ratings, awards, dog-friendly or any other special facilities/features when a venue or accommodation has specifically advised it. We apologise for any omissions, and welcome updates and useful information for our future guides. Please email updates@coolcanalsguides.com

Some of the best - Quick finder

Holiday hireboats

The rush hour is a distant concept as you push off from the banks letting yourself unwind on the water. Boating holidays are all about waking to the sounds of water and nature, slow travel, long lunches, gentle sightseeing and boaty camaraderie. Lazy summers simply messing about in boats. You can make your holiday extra healthy by taking bikes or walking boots with you. Sleep peacefully with water reflecting through your cabin porthole then, after a hearty breakfast on board, spend part of your day walking or cycling and the rest drifting peacefully along in your narrowboat or barge until dusk and it's time to moor up again (and snuggle up in the local pub). Cruise and stop wherever you choose, it's all about taking charge of your own tiller, getting woolly and rugged handling ropes and mastering fancy knot work, losing yourself in the pleasure of slow boating. Navigating water roads brings you so close to nature you can't help but connect with elements you've forgotten since childhood. Go sightseeing in style.

Hire a narrowboat

Narrow canals were built for narrowboats and these aptly named romantic boats are the real reason canals have remained navigable and virtually unchanged for over 200 years; but don't worry about the 21st-century basics of electricity and water because modern hire boats are like floating cottages with all the homely comforts of central heating, carpets, fully equipped kitchens, shower and TV.

Handling the boat

It doesn't matter if you've never been on a narrowboat before, learning how to steer with a tiller and handle ropes is all part of the fun. Crewing a boat is teamwork with something for everyone to do. It may sound corny but getting away from it all in the confines of a boat, mixed with the freedom of an enforced outdoor experience, really can bring families together in a special way. Working the locks is fun. The occasional cog is stiff to turn, but most can be operated even by the kids. Your hireboat company will give you all necessary instructions to sail safely, but if you are nervous book on a helmsman course before your holiday.

Details:
RYA Inland Waterways Helmsman's Course www.ryatraining.org

Planning the route

Narrowboat hire centres are all over Britain. It's a good idea to bear in mind how many locks you want to encounter on your journey; although more heavily locked canals are fascinating, for some people they can become exhausting to a point beyond fun. When planning your route, an approximate time measure to follow is 3mph, adding 10 minutes per lock. See some of our favourite cruising rings on the following page and our top 10 canals on page 236.

Where to cruise?

Canals are linear and it's true that cruising from A to B can be a fascinatingly different view if embarked on the return from B to A. Different canals linked in the network can also provide circular routes called 'rings'.

Five of our favourite cruising rings:

Cheshire Ring

A journey capturing the pulse of metropolitan Manchester, slicing through the city's canalside gay village and swanning off into stunning views of the Peak District, with scrambles up Pennine inclines and falls down into river valleys. Stop off and explore the amazing Anderton Boat Lift, one of the 7 Wonders of the waterways.

Details:
Ashton Canal, Macclesfield Canal, Peak Forest Canal, Rochdale Canal, Trent & Mersey Canal and Bridgewater Canal. Allow 2 weeks for comfort.
Further info:
Anderton Boat Lift (see page 38 & 243).

South Pennine Ring

For the hardy, the rewards await. Recent restoration has reopened a route spectacularly traversing the Pennines, blessing boaters with a remarkable journey that includes not only the northern heights of spectacular scenery but also a 3½-hour journey underground, cutting 17,094 feet through the Pennines in the Standedge Tunnel - the longest, deepest and highest tunnel in the country and one of the 7 Wonders of the waterways.

Details:
Ashton Canal, Calder & Hebble Navigation, Huddersfield Narrow Canal and Rochdale Canal. 3 weeks happy (but energetic) cruising.
Further info:
Standedge Tunnel needs prebooking (see page 38 & 243).

Stourport Ring

One of the most popular rings with plenty of locks to keep you busy. This cruising ring gambols through Birmingham and rolls on beyond into some of the greenest pastures in the heart of England.

Details:
Worcester & Birmingham Canal, Staffordshire & Worcestershire Canal and River Severn. 2 weeks leisurely cruising but can be done in 1 week if you do 8 hours cruising a day.
Further info:
Stourport is the only town in the UK specifically built for the canals.

Avon Ring

A mix of canal and river navigation travelling through the rural delights of Evesham, meeting the heritage of Worcester and Stratford-upon-Avon and taking in the longest lock flight of all: the infamous Tardebigge Flight.

Details:
River Severn, River Avon, Worcester & Birmingham Canal and Stratford-upon-Avon Canal. 2 weeks comfortable cruising allowing time to stop off.
Further info:
Extra licence required for the river Avon.

Four Counties Ring

The big adventure is to cross the borders and take in the best of Staffordshire, Shropshire, Cheshire and the West Midlands. It's a slog up Heartbreak Hill but keep yours eyes peeled for the views and brace yourself for the infamous Harecastle Tunnel (2926 yards long).

Details:
Shropshire Union Canal, Staffordshire & Worcestershire Canal and Trent & Mersey Canal. 2 weeks cruising at around 5 hours cruising a day.
Further info:
The original Harecastle Tunnel built by James Brindley in 1777 was replaced by the current tunnel by Thomas Telford in 1827 (see page 245). Huge doors close behind you to allow giant ventilation fans to operate as you cruise through.

Luxury boat hire

Narrowboating can sometimes be about getting bohemian and close to nature but that doesn't mean you can't spoil yourself with luxuries too. Many hireboat companies offer supreme boats with 5-star ratings from the Tourist Board. The price tag can be higher but with it comes plush cruising and all onboard frivolities from gadgets in the galley to WI-FI.

Moonraker

Moonraker's luxury 5-star widebeam boats on the Kennet & Avon Canal are breaking the rules of canal boating. They're chic, decadent and stylish with summer decks, cosy night-time stoves and all the naughtiness of a Jacuzzi.

Details:
Moonraker Narrowboat Company T:07973 876891 www.moonboats.co.uk
Location:
By bridge 173, Bradford on Avon. Kennet & Avon Canal OS ST815604
Further info:
5-star luxury boats

Maestermyn

Maestermyn Cruisers also offer boats for one-upmanship. When you want that special champagne moment, a floating four-poster is guaranteed to impress. And this boating holiday indulges you with a whirlpool bath and sexy lighting, even spoiling you with chocolates and flowers on arrival.

Details:
Maestermyn Cruisers T:01691 662424 www.maestermyn.co.uk
Location:
By Maestermyn Bridge (no.5), Whittington. Llangollen Canal OS SJ353325
Further info:
Romantic Lady & Romantic Princess special 2-person boats

And more...

ABC Leisure Group:
Alvechurch Boats, Viking Afloat, Red Line
Boats & Wessex Narrowboats. 11 bases
T:0845 1264098 www.ukboathire.com

Anglo Welsh Waterway Holidays:
9 bases across the UK
T:0117 3041122 www.anglowelsh.co.uk

Black Prince Narrowboat Holidays:
6 bases across the UK
T:01527 575115 www.black-prince.com

Drifters:
A collection of the country's leading
independent boating holiday companies
T:0844 9840322 www.drifters.co.uk

Beacon Park Boats:
Monmouthshire & Brecon Canal
T:01873 858277 www.beaconparkboats.com

Rose Narrowboats:
Oxford Canal
T:01788 832449 www.rose-narrowboats.co.uk

Napton Narrowboats:
Shropshire Union & Oxford Canals
T:01926 813644 www.napton-marina.co.uk

Shire Cruisers:
Calder & Hebble Navigation & Rochdale Canal
T:01422 832712 www.shirecruisers.co.uk

Andersen Boats:
Trent & Mersey Canal
T:01606 833668 www.andersenboats.com

For a comprehensive listing of all hireboat
companies in UK: www.coolcanalsguides.com

Day boats

Do something really different on your day off. Go boating. Canals were of course created with narrowboats and barges in mind, but boats of all shapes and colours go out to play on today's leisurely waterways - cruisers, sailing ships, yachts, wide barges and more. You can hire a small narrowboat, catch the city waterbus, chill out on a trip boat or even step back in time on a horse-drawn boat ride. Stop for a picnic, call in at a canalside pub, sightsee, shop, slow down and have fun. Get away from it all. Escape on the water.

Horse-drawn boats

Take a horse-drawn boat trip and let your imagination drift effortlessly back in time to a slower pace and quieter ways, as you glide along on the water with genuine horsepower. You can forget all about noisy engines when the silence is broken only by hooves clopping in unhurried rhythm. Downwind the smell of horse is ridiculously romantic. Soak up the scenery and let stress slip away, but spare a thought for the hardships these gentle giants endured during the industrial heyday of the canals. The strain of tugging heavy cargoes is evident today and if you look closely you'll sometimes see rope marks gouged into brickwork along the canals. Tourism must be kinder to these beautiful horses as they seem to plod effortlessly along in need of only occasional cajolery and a few tasty treats to keep them going. Gazing from the boat, you might spot walkers, cyclists or fishermen on the towpaths, but the truth is towpaths traditionally belonged to the horse. Whether you ride in the boat or walk alongside the horse - it's an experience not to miss.

Horse-drawn boats have become a rare sight on modern canals, with only five still operating commercially on the networks:

Tiverton Canal Company
Details: T:01884 253345 www.tivertoncanal.co.uk
The Wharf, Tiverton. Grand Western Canal OS SS963123

Horse Drawn Boats
Details: T:01978 860702 www.horsedrawnboats.co.uk
Llangollen Wharf. Llangollen Canal OS SJ214422

Bywater Holiday Cruises
Details: T:07971 303416 www.bywaterholidays.co.uk
Holiday cruises along middle section of the Montgomery Canal

Kennet Horse Boat Company
Details: T:01488 658866 www.kennet-horse-boat.co.uk
Kintbury. Kennet & Avon Canal OS SU385671

Godalming Packetboat Company
Details: T:01483 414938 www.horseboat.org.uk
Godalming Wharf. River Wey Navigations OS SU974441

Hire a boat for a day

If the waterways are the 'fastest way to slow down', and you've only got a day to escape the humdrum and stress of everyday life, then hiring a boat is the perfect outdoor escape. Taste the independence of getting away from it all with a breeze in your face and nothing to clutter your mind except the challenge of handling a boat. Even when you're only going for a day you don't need to worry if you've never steered a boat before, learning is all part of the fun, and even the kids can have a go. Day hire boats can be anything from large narrowboats to small motor boats. Boat centres are scattered all around the canal networks, so you can hire in a place that suits you and some boats are available all year round. When you are out for only a day, it's especially worth considering the number of locks you might encounter as they can take 15 minutes to work through and some heavily locked canals can be exhausting. A day out in a boat isn't only about the boat: it's travel that brings you face to face with the unexpected. Wildlife, and nature, customs and culture of the waterways communities, heritage and all the secrets of a hidden water world. Being alone in the company of slow waters is a detox for the mind and forces you to unwind. If you want to, you can stop off in the middle of nowhere for a picnic lunch, or cruise round the next bend and pull up at a canalside inn. It's a day of refreshingly simple choices. Seize the day, get afloat.

Further info:
It's possible to hire a small boat for a day or half a day on most canals. A couple of our favourites are:

Anglo Welsh Waterway Holidays:
9 bases across the UK including Great Haywood on the Staffordshire & Worcestershire Canal and Trevor Basin on the Llangollen Canal. T:0117 3041122 www.anglowelsh.co.uk
Snaygill Boats:
Based in Skipton on the Leeds & Liverpool Canal T:01756 795150 www.snaygillboats.co.uk

For detailed information on all canals across the UK and boat companies offering boats for day hire, visit www.waterscape.com

Trip boats

Climb aboard a trip boat and let trained crew, with headfuls of knowledge, take you on a journey of discovery into the world of the waterways.

Dragonfly

Sit back and relax for a few hours while the Dragonfly takes you on a cruise along the Monmouthshire & Brecon Canal. The crew are genuinely friendly and the route meanders the mountainside with heart-singing views.

Details:
Dragonfly Cruises, Brecon, Mon & Brec Canal. T:07831 685222 www.dragonfly-cruises.co.uk
Bar. Wheelchair lift.

Kennet & Avon Canal Trust

Trip boats that are in no hurry as they cruise the tranquil water near Bath. The Kennet & Avon Canal Trust operate three trip boats and also offer special charter trips.

Details:
Kennet & Avon Canal Trust T:01380 721279 www.katrust.org. One boat has a wheelchair lift.

Falkirk Wheel

The Falkirk Wheel is an iconic millennium masterpiece and offers an unforgettable boat trip. Climb aboard for an hour-long epic cruise into the wheel, and rise elegantly from the Forth & Clyde Canal 115 feet to meet the Union Canal. The Falkirk visitor centre is free and pads a great day out with plenty to grab the kids' interest.

Details:
Falkirk Wheel. 08700 500208 www.thefalkirkwheel.co.uk (see also page 243) Disabled access good

Themed trip boats

Boat operators creatively come up with all sorts of themed boat trips ranging from Santa to cream teas! See pages 145 & 149 for more details.

Anderton Boat Lift

The Anderton Boat lift is impressive enough from the ground but you can enjoy a 30-minute boat trip and get a boat's eye view from inside the lift. The Edwin Clarke is a glass-topped trip boat taking you 50 feet up from the River Weaver to the Trent & Mersey Canal above. The boat masters are waterways oracles willingly answering any questions about the lift. To complete the day there's a visitor centre, exhibition area, café and gift shop.

Details:
Anderton Boat Lift T:01606 786777 www.andertonboatlift.co.uk One of the 7 Wonders of the waterways (see page 243). Good disabled access.

Pontcysyllte

The boat trip that comes close to flying in a narrowboat. The Thomas Telford cruises the Llangollen Canal with the highlight of crossing the Pontcysyllte Aqueduct. Seating is inside the narrowboat with clear window views if you dare look. Luckily for the vertiginous there's a well-stocked bar onboard.

Details:
Llangollen Wharf T:01978 860702 www.horsedrawnboats.co.uk One of the 7 Wonders of the waterways (see page 243)

Standedge Tunnel and Visitor Centre

No boat is allowed to travel the tunnel under its own power and so electric tugboats tow all narrowboats through this tunnel under the Pennines. It's a convoy of excitement and resilience as they set off for a 3-hour journey into the highest, longest, deepest tunnel in the country. For an adventurous day out, take a through trip on the tug and then walk back over the top in the high air of the Pennines.

Details:
Standedge Tunnel & Visitor Centre T:01484 844298 www.standedge.co.uk One of the 7 Wonders of the waterways (see page 243). Shorter trips in glass-roofed boats also operate. No dogs. Disabled access to glass-roofed boat trips and Visitor Centre but no access on the through tunnel trip.

Catch the bus

London

Take a one-way trip between Camden Lock and Little Venice. Can include entrance to London Zoo with your ticket, or go on one of their special day trips.

Further info:
London Waterbus Company
T:020 7482 2660 www.londonwaterbus.co.uk
Location:
Camden Lock, London.
Regent's Canal OS TQ286840

Birmingham

Catch the waterbus in the heart of Birmingham's canals to the Mailbox, Gas Street Basin and Brindley Place for shopping, food or culture. See pages 195-197 for more details.

Further info:
Sherborne Wharf Waterbus:
T:0121 4556163 www.sherbornewharf.co.uk
Location:
Sherborne Wharf, Birmingham.
Worcs & Birmingham Canal OS SP060867

Paddles and oars

Paddle across aqueducts, venture into forgotten waterways where other boats can't reach. Explore landlocked and forgotten canals away from the main tourist boat rings. Stop for lunch at the pub, or picnic amongst wild flora on the canal bank. If it's excitement you're after, get out on the canals in a canoe this summer. It's definitely not white water, knuckle-clenching stuff and doesn't unexpectedly turn into canoe-slalom as rivers might, so paddlers of any age, size and shape can enjoy the kind waters of canals. For even slower fun, you can hire a rowing boat to wibble away and laze about, leaving the inhibitions of the 9 to 5 world behind. Whether you choose to pick up oars or paddles, part of the thrill is breathing in fresh air with no engine to spoil the sounds of nature. Discover the gentle ride out on the open water road taking you to secret hideaways and some breathtaking scenery.

Go canoeing

Canoeing on the canals is for anyone from beginners to marathon paddlers, in canoes or kayaks to more laid-back open Canadian canoes. Safe for families and novices, the adventurous can tour the open water road between dusk and dawn, with the freedom of over 2,000 water miles to explore. Head for Scottish or Welsh waters, following wild Celtic water trails or just launch on your local canal. If you don't own your own canoe, you can always hire one. The majority of canoe hire centres tend to be on rivers; however, the British Canoe Union (see page 47) will be able to advise the nearest centre to the canal you want to visit.

Our favourite canals for canoeing:
Monmouthshire & Brecon Canal, Lancaster Canal, Kennet & Avon Canal and Llangollen Canal

Devizes to Westminster International Canoe Race

It's the longest nonstop canoe race in the world. Every year since 1948 on Easter weekend, a frenzy of canoes sets off from Devizes in Wiltshire racing 125 miles to Westminster Bridge in London (52 miles on the Kennet & Avon Canal, 55 miles on the River Thames with the final stretch on the tidal Thames). The race is tough, based on skill, stamina and, frankly, complete madness. It's a challenge with reputation! Luckily, if you're not an experienced canoeist there are different categories from nonstop racing to noncompetitive paddling over 4 days. So if you're a beginner, get training. And why not enter the race for charity?

Start: Devizes OS SU004618 Finish: Westminster Bridge OS TQ305796
Details:
International Canoe Race T:0118 9665912 www.dwrace.org.uk
Further info:
Organised and run entirely by volunteers. All entrants should be members of the British Canoe Union www.bcu.org.uk

And more...

Canals can be safe waters for beginners and there are only a few rules to bear in mind:

Check with British Waterways for licences and permissions required on individual waterways

British Canoe Union (BCU) membership includes a licence to canoe on all canals owned by British Waterways

Wear a life jacket

Go in a group of 3 or more for added safety (one of the group should hold a British Canoe Union BCU star qualification)

Navigate to the right and give way to motorized craft (it's easier to turn a canoe quickly than great lengths of narrowboat metal)

Don't canoe through tunnels

Never stay in your canoe in a working lock

It makes sense to avoid canals with a lot of locks. Waterscape has relevant info on every canal (see below)

British Canoe Union:
www.bcu.org.uk

British Waterways:
www.britishwaterways.co.uk

Waterscape:
www.waterscape.com

Go for a walk

You can't get lost, just follow the water. But don't be fooled, canal walks aren't just for softies. Whether you stroll a slow water-mile, hike a full canal or go on a waterside backpacking holiday, these rambles can be big and beautiful and as different as any far-off place. Don't expect the predictable; every canal has its own story to tell and contours to explore. Waterways walks are not just about walking: you're travelling back in time following historic trade routes rambling ingeniously through mountains, hills, Areas of Outstanding Natural Beauty, National Parks and every green edge of Britain. It's a great water escape on foot. As soon as you scramble down onto the towpaths almost anywhere on Britain's canals, you experience the unrivalled peace and solitude of a landscape steeped in wild aromas of air and water, chirpings of nature and the charisma of an unchanged place hidden from the outside world. Walk by water, enjoy the outdoors, be neighbourly to boaters, feel at peace with the small things in life. The ultimate free pleasure. No fuss, just pull on comfy shoes and go for a walk.

Brecon Beacons canal walk

The views smell Welsh and there is genuine wow factor on this waterside walk. Treading in the company of mountains, your eyes touch the peaks of Pen y Fan and Sugar Loaf, and yet this high hill trail is never more than an easy canalside walk. So it's fun whether your boots are well waxed or you're new to walking. Most of the route paces parallel to the River Usk in the valley below and views never really stop teasing through the trees. There are several lift bridges and Brynich Lock, an award-winning lock perfumed by flowers, is worth dawdling over. Then, just around the corner, Brynich Aqueduct stylishly carries the canal over the river. Just past bridge 160, the highlight of the canal demands a gasp at the open views around Pen y Fan. In contrast, Talybont reminds you of the past with limestone kilns and a tram road that once linked the canal to the quarries and coalfields of South Wales' industrial valleys. The Mon & Brec is a tree-lined water trail through the heart of the Brecon Beacons National Park, with sweeps of high air to blow cobwebs from your head and feed your very soul!

Start: OS SO046281 Finish: OS SO115225 Monmouthshire & Brecon Canal
Eat and drink:
Tipple & Tiffin, Brecon Basin T:01874 611866 www.theatrbrycheiniog.co.uk
Royal Oak, Pencelli (By bridge 153) T:01874 665396
White Hart Inn,Talybont-on-Usk (By bridge 143) T:01874 676227 www.breconbunkhouse.co.uk
Star Inn, Talybont-on-Usk (By the aqueduct) T:01874 676635 www.starinntalybont.co.uk
Traveller's Rest, Talybont-on-Usk (By bridge 142) T:01874 676233 www.travellersrestinn.com
Further info:
Monmouthshire, Brecon & Abergavenny Canals Trust www.mon-brec-canal-trust.org.uk
More info on Monmouthshire & Brecon Canal and other canals - www.waterscape.com
Make a weekend of it and sleep at Pencelli campsite (see page 162)
Secrets of the past
Watch out for rusty signposts peeping over many of the bridges on the Mon and Brec. A world without cars seems inconceivable today, yet of course canals preceded our beloved speedy carbon-burning noise polluters. With the arrival of the motor engine, new pressures were put on canal bridges originally only constructed for foot passengers or horse and cart. These signs warned drivers of newfangled motor vehicles to beware of the weight limit of up to 5 tons.

Pennine canal way

Mention the Pennines and woolly walkers with thermos flasks, cheese sandwiches, rosy cheeks, soggy maps and scuffed boots probably spring to mind. Canals cross the Pennines with much less hoo-ha than other paths in these parts. Tie up your bootlaces and set off on foot; it's a civilized journey with something very special around every corner. Skipton is the 'gateway to the Yorkshire Dales' and any journey along the Leeds & Liverpool Canal is the perfect way to leave the crowds behind and detox from the mayhem. The Pennine Way, the path serious walkers covet, crosses the canal at Gargrave, just west of Skipton. The 17-mile stretch of the Leeds & Liv rambling between Gargrave and Bingley Five Rise Locks, one of the 7 wonders of the waterways (see page 243), is easy going, seductively wandering through quiet green landscape scattered with idyllic villages. It's a hardy walker's right of passage to tread the geography of this part of the world and the ease of the towpath trail makes it accessible to almost anyone! Don't be put off in winter either: cold air on the water can be sublime. Whenever you go there's the promise of a perfect day and stepping along this section of the Leeds & Liverpool Canal in Yorkshire is the real thing for crowd-free water therapy.

Start: OS SD934545 Finish: OS SE107399 Leeds & Liverpool Canal
Eat and drink:
The Narrow Boat, Skipton (In town) T:01756 797922 www.markettowntaverns.co.uk
Herriots Hotel, Skipton (By bridge 176) T:01756 792781 www.herriotsforleisure.co.uk
The White Lion,Kildwick (Canalside by bridge 186) T:01535 632265
Bridge Inn, Silsden (Canalside by bridge 191A) T:01535 653144
Five Rise Locks Café & Store, Bingley (Top of locks) T:01274 562221
Look out for:
The memorial to 7 Polish airmen whose bomber crashed into the canal at Bradley in 1943.
It's also worth walking an extra 2½ miles beyond Bingley to Saltaire World Heritage Site (see page 245)
www.saltairevillage.info
Further info:
Leeds & Liverpool Canal Society www.llcs.org.uk
More info on Leeds & Liverpool Canal and other canals - www.waterscape.com

Kinver walk

Scan any map of England and the grey urban mass in the middle might not scream out as good walking territory: but canals have a way of surprising us. A closer look reveals a secretly dramatic waterway with great scenery defying its proximity to the maddening crowds. A slice of pure tranquillity, a miraculous retreat from the nearby material sprawl, with leafy waters, caves and mighty red sandstone rocks perilously overhanging the water. The Staffordshire & Worcestershire Canal is a stunner. Walk from Wolverley to Stewponey and you won't find any negative references to the ever-nearby urban borders. Hyde Lock nestles above Kinver village looking down from a woodland oasis and could rival anywhere on the canals of England for chocolate box status.

Start: OS SO831791 Finish: OS SO861848 Staffordshire & Worcestershire Canal

Eat and drink:
The Lock Inn, Wolverley (By Wolverley Lock) T:01562 850581
The Old Smithy Tearooms, Wolverley (By Wolverley Lock - also run by the Lock Inn)
Whittington Inn (300yds from bridge 28) T:01384 872110 (Reputedly built in the 14th century by Dick Whittington's grandfather)
The Vine, Kinver (By Kinver Lock) T:01384 877291 www.thevineinnkinver.co.uk
(Pulls nectareous real ale from the local Enville Brewery!)

Look out for:
Debdale Lock: an intriguing small cave, once chiselled into the rock to provide overnight stabling for working boat horses.
Cookley Tunnel: cottages perched above it appear as if built into the tunnel arch.
Austcliff Rock: juts out over the canal, menacing the paintwork of shiny boats.
Hyde Lock: wafting a golden canopy in autumn and bleating with bluebells in spring.
Stewponey Lock: quirky octagonal toll house.
Boundary stone: marks the boundary between Staffordshire and Worcestershire.
Detour to Kinver Edge, National Trust land, for windswept walks and views as far as the Cotswolds on a clear day. Fascinating cave houses dug into the soft red sandstone of this area were lived in up until the 1950s. Holy Austin Cave House is one of the houses restored to give visitors some insight into Victorian life as a cave dweller. www.nationaltrust.org.uk

Further info:
Staffs & Worcs Canal Society www.swcs.org.uk
More info on Staffs & Worcs Canal and other canals - www.waterscape.com

Wild Scottish coast to coast

More than just a walk. Pull on your boots and expect nothing less than goose bumps. Make a holiday of it and stride the Caledonian Canal coast to coast through unspoilt scenery from the capital of the west Highlands, Fort William, all the way to Inverness on the east coast. The canal swells into lochs and narrows back into canal again, rambling 60 Highland miles with literally breathtaking surroundings and even views of Ben Nevis. Look out for Neptune's Staircase, a spectacular flight of 8 locks not to be missed. You'll pass the beautiful Loch Lochy and Loch Oich, and watch out, you could find yourself unexpectedly walking in the company of strangers on the banks of Loch Ness! Unlike the narrow canals and narrowboats of central England, boats on the Caledonian are grander, with the sea in mind. The Caledonian is the quickest sailing route from the North Sea to the Atlantic Ocean and Irish Sea. It's an inland waterway route, flinging Highland landscapes between edges of wilder water. Nature won't leave you alone and the spirit of many clan battles whistle in the wind too. No one comes away from this walk untouched.

Start: OS NN096766 Finish: OS NH644467 Caledonian Canal
Eat and drink:
Lochy Bar (300yds from Neptune's Staircase) T:01397 703587 www.thelochy.co.uk
Moorings Hotel (By Neptune's Staircase) T:01397 772797 www.moorings-fortwilliam.co.uk
Bridge House Tea Garden, Aberchalder (Canalside by Loch Oich) T:01809 501302
Thistle Stop Cafe, Aberchalder (800yds from canal) T:01809 501478
Eagle Barge Pub (Moored by Laggan Locks) T:07789 858567 www.theeaglebarge.com
Boathouse Restaurant, Fort Augustus T:01320 366682 www.lochnessboathouse.co.uk
Bothy Restaurant & Bar, Fort Augustus T:01320 366710 www.lochnessrestaurant.co.uk
Fiddlers' Restaurant/Coffee Shop, Drumnadrochit T:01456 450678 www.fiddledrum.co.uk
Look out for:
Neptune's Staircase: a dramatic flight of locks
Urquhart Castle near Drumnadrochit: on a point jutting out into Loch Ness
Moy Swing Bridge: the only surviving original cast-iron bridge on the canal
Views of Ben Nevis and Nessie (the monster, of course!)
Further info:
Official route and information on the Great Glen Way www.greatglenway.com
Scottish Inland Waterways' Association www.siwa.org.uk
More info on Caledonian Canal and other canals - www.waterscape.com

And more...

Extreme walks

Forget the Munros - why not go canalbagging? Walk the entire length of any canal and start ticking them off your 'baggers' list.

Walk coast to coast

Scotland: Caledonian Canal
North: Leeds & Liverpool Canal
South: Kennet & Avon Canal

City to city

Birmingham to London along the Grand Union Canal

In a circle

Some of the boat cruising rings make great walking (see page 24-25)

Further info:
Visit our website for highlights of our challenge to walk every canal in the UK
www.coolcanalsguides.com

The Ramblers' Association have a list of canal towpath walks across the country
www.ramblers.org.uk

Go for a bike ride

Imagine a place where you can cycle all day and never meet a car, you don't have to struggle up hills and the views are to die for. Add an idyllic splash of water to the scene and you're pedalling the canals of Britain. Towpaths, originally designed for horses, make perfect bike trails. Slow down from the crazy race, shrug off the 4x4 armour, and instead feel the freedom of two wheels with the wind in your face. You can travel at your own pace to discover new sights – so whether you want to tour coast to coast on the Caledonian Canal in the Highlands of Scotland, or pootle along your local waterway, it's the ultimate way to touch tranquillity. Go alone, or take the kids and let them ride safely in the great outdoors with all the thrill of a stress-free adventure following a secluded historic trail.

Family cycle ride

The Kennet & Avon Canal rolls from Bristol to Reading, oozing Roman charm and Wiltshire magic. The 12 miles from Bradford on Avon to Devizes have been especially improved with wheels in mind (bikes, buggies and wheelchairs). The towpath is well surfaced and wide, and has oodles of 'bikes welcome' ethos, making a great family-friendly ride. This day ride starts at Bradford on Avon, one of Wiltshire's beauty spots, often described as a miniature Bath. The canalside Lock Inn Café offers bike hire of every imaginable kind with child seats, trailer buggies, tandems, adult and child bikes, and you can even grab a belly-bursting 'Boatman's Breakfast' before you set off. The route is a peaceful trail untouched by time; a haven for wildlife, alive with narrowboats and, in keeping with the area, canal architecture is aesthetically constructed from local stone. The highlight of the ride is Caen Hill Locks, one of the 7 wonders of the waterways (see page 243). Above the flight awaits a picturesque canalside tea shop and it's worth moseying into Devizes to have a look round the small museum shop and have an ice cream before you experience the canal from a different viewpoint on the return ride. A guaranteed whinge free, healthy, eco-friendly day out with all the freedom and adventure kids love.

Start: OS ST825603 Finish: OS SU004617 Kennet & Avon Canal
Eat and drink:
Lock Inn Café T:01225 868068 www.thelockinn.co.uk
Canal Tavern (Opposite Lock Inn Café) T:01225 867426
Wharf Cottage (By Bradford Lock) Kennet & Avon Canal Trust T:01225 868683
Granny Mo's Tea Room (By Bradford Lock) T:01225 867515 www.grannymos.co.uk
Barge Inn, Seend (By lock no.19) T:01380 828230
Caen Hill Café, Devizes (By lock no.44) T:01452 318000 Dog-friendly
Look out for:
Great Tithe Barn, Bradford on Avon - one of the finest examples in England, just before Lock Inn
Original start of Wiltshire & Berkshire Canal, now long abandoned, at Semington Wharf
Caen Hill Locks
Further info:
This ride is part of National Route 4 of the National Cycle Network (see page 69)
Bike hire: Adult bike £12.00 & Child bike/Trailer buggy/Trailer bike £8.00 Child seat £6.00
Kennet & Avon Canal Trust www.katrust.org.uk
Kennet & Avon Canal Museum & Shop, Devizes T:01380 729489
More info on Caen Hill, Kennet & Avon Canal and other canals - www.waterscape.com

Llangollen to Pontcysyllte

It's only a short day's ride but pack your toothbrush, you'll want to stay.
A handful of water miles cram enough excitement to fill a holiday. High
above town, Llangollen Wharf is usually busy with boats, people and
horses but follow the towpath out of town and you'll discover a lonelier
landscape with only sheep, herons and soaring kite for company. For a
while the canal is dramatically only wide enough for one boat, and anything
less than nifty boat steering can ricochet a bumper spectacle for the
passer-by. Beyond the visitors' moorings, both canal and towpath widen
as glorious views spread out ahead. An enticing bench, a lift bridge, then
a curve in the canal breaks into spectacular views over the River Dee in
its valley below. This is a great picnic spot with a birds-eye-view of boats
slowly wending their way along the narrow passage. Once you've dragged
yourself away, your next temptation is the Sun Trevor pub above bridge 41.
The canal continues its narrow way past sheep-filled fields, trees and under
pretty stone bridges until you reach Trevor Basin where there's boat hire,
café and shop. Brace yourself as the outrageous Pontcysyllte Aqueduct
awaits. You're in for an extreme experience. It's pure adrenalin. Dismount
to brave the slim towpath hugging the water with 127-foot sheer drops
either side. Halfway across you'll grasp why it's officially one of the seven
wonders of the waterways (see page 243).

Start: OS SJ214422 Finish: OS SJ270422 Llangollen Canal
Eat and drink:
Tea Room & Gift shop, Llangollen Wharf T:01978 860702 www.horsedrawnboats.co.uk
Sun Trevor, Sun Bank (Overlooking bridge 41) T:01978 860651 www.suntrevor.co.uk
Telford Inn, Trevor Basin (Canalside in the Basin) T:01978 820469
Aqueduct Inn, Froncysyllte (View towards Pontcysyllte Aqueduct) T:01691 772481
Look out for:
Llangollen Wharf - the horse-drawn boat trips (see page 35) set off from here
River Dee in the valley below you as you cycle
Trevor Basin with its boats and Pontcysyllte Aqueduct
Further info:
For safety reasons, dismount before crossing the Aqueduct.
Shropshire Union Canal Society (inc. Llangollen Canal) www.shropshireunion.org.uk
More info on Pontcysyllte, Llangollen Canal and other canals - www.waterscape.com
For more information on Llangollen and the area, see pages 201-207

Cycle cruise in the Scottish Highlands

High on Tartan air, it's a week-long cruise through heather-banked lochs and canals mixed with pumped-up cycling and hearty Scottish food. Scottish Highlander, a 117-foot barge from the fleet of GoBarging, offers charter groups for 6 to 8 passengers to enjoy the freedom of combining touring by bike with luxury boating and sublime Scottish scenery. On board the Scottish Highlander a cheery crew tend to your every need after adrenalin-powered days cycling the Great Glen Cycle Route. The barge even comes with its own floating Master Chef to cook for you; and it's not fast food on offer with seductive Scottish-sounding creations such as 'Munro of marinated salmon'. Evenings afloat over Scottish gourmet dinners are about food, washed down with malt whisky, cheese and wine, all digested in the good company of your surroundings. Start the days with breakfast on board, and then follow an itinerary pedalling between 17 and 25 miles each day. Cycle head up with views of Ben Nevis one day and head down in case you bump into old Nessie the next. Follow the Great Glen Cycle Route coast to coast, through hills and forest, alongside the Caledonian Canal and around the legendary lochs. Cruise through Neptune's Staircase of Locks. Visit a whisky distillery. Go shopping in Fort William. It's a big boat-bike combo and definitely a holiday with a difference.

Start: OS NH653458 Finish: OS NN115772 Caledonian Canal
Eat and drink:
On board
Look out for:
The knowledgeable crew are on hand to tell you what to look for and when!
Further info:
Scottish Highlander Cycling Cruise from Inverness to Fort William
For charter groups of 6-8 passengers T:01784 482439 www.gobarging.com
More info on Caledonian Canal and other canals - www.waterscape.com

Useful info

Cycling permit
You will need a cycling permit to cycle some towpaths owned by British Waterways. Permits are free and easily obtained from their website.

Waterways and Towpath Code
London has its own Towpath Code of Conduct. It's a good idea to be familiar with the general Waterways Code.

Seasonal tips
In early spring, towpaths are prepared for the start of the boating season. At this time of year, hedge cutting can leave spiky debris from hawthorn that can be lethal for tyres (using protective tyre liners works for us). Winter on the canals is the quietest time and can be a great escape on two wheels in all weathers but take into account that some formerly smooth or grassy surfaces can transform into a muddy quagmire in heavy rain.

General info
Waterscape gives general info about individual canals and provides a useful list (free to download) of all towpaths suitable for cycling.

Waterways Code www.britishwaterways.co.uk
Cycle permits, London's Code, general canal information and suitable towpaths
www.waterscape.com

Enjoy the culture
Canal towpaths are a slow zone and nobody welcomes speeding bikes. Racing isn't the point anyway.

Sustrans
As a perfect car-free environment, many towpaths are part of the National Cycle Network co-ordinated by Sustrans. Find out more about Sustrans and which networks link up with the canals on their website.

www.sustrans.org.uk

Slow food

Food is inseparable from canal culture and since nothing is going to hurry on the waterways, it's not just slow food, it's slow eating too. Gastronomy is no different to anything else on the water – it can't be bullied into fuss or rush. Alfresco lunches to linger over, lazy teas in the afternoon sun, food for free plucked from the hedgerows, canalside inns and food afloat (on narrowboats, barges and any shape of boat you can think of) stir special flavours for slow eating. Canals are full of surprises when it comes to food!

Organics

Good food isn't necessarily the most expensively bought nor exotically prepared. It's the whole process that counts: where ingredients originally come from, how they're grown, cooked and presented. Monstrously perfect fruit and veg shrink-wrapped to suffocation, ready meals e-numbered to death, meat produced without compassion and anything hauled via an unfair trade market across the globe, gobbling gastro airmiles galore, cannot be good food. Like anywhere else in Britain, on today's canals you'll find good and not so good food but fresh, ethical and organic food has a strong place in canal life.

Details:
The Soil Association is the leading campaigning and certification organisation in the UK for organic food and farming. Their consumer website gives comprehensive info about organic food and its searchable directory includes shops and accommodation. www.whyorganic.org www.soilassociation.org
Further info:
The National Farmers' Retail & Markets Association (FARMA) is a co-operative of farmers, local scale producers and farmers' market organisers. www.farma.org.uk To find farm shops or farmers' markets by the canals, visit www.farmshopping.net or www.farmersmarkets.net and visit www.pickyourown.info for farms where you can pick your own fruit and vegetables.

Floating Farm Shop

If you want to leave supermarket shopping trolleys behind and head for more ethical climes, visit a farm shop. Snuggled along the waterside on the Oxford Canal is an unusual narrowboat farm shop. Run as part of its owner's compact good-life, produce is sold aboard 'Pan', the narrowboat, moored alongside a fully organic smallholding with free-range hens, a few dairy cattle and a tiny seasonal market garden. Go on a Sunday and treat yourself to one of the farm's fab cream teas too. This farm shop knows nothing of corporate swindling and capitalist manners: if nobody is on hand with friendly assistance, just serve yourself and use the honesty box.

Details:
Floating Farm Shop T:07837 362683
Location:
Above Pigeon Lock (no.39), Kirtlington. Oxford Canal OS SP488194

Away2dine

Away2dine is a cruising restaurant narrowboat operating all year round. The boat's floodlights illuminate the evening canals during its 3-hour dinner cruises and they also do Sunday Roast special cruises.

Details:
Away2dine T:0845 6445244 www.away2dine.co.uk Also available for corporate or private charter
Location:
The Mailbox, Birmingham. Worcester & Birmingham Canal OS SP064863

Judith Mary II

Deemed fit for a princess when Princess Diana ate on her during a visit to the Peak District in 1990, this luxury restaurant boat operates all year taking diners on 2½-hour cruises along the Peak Forest Canal.

Details: Judith Mary II T:01663 734737 www.trafalgarmarineservices.co.uk/restaurantboat
Location:
Whaley Bridge. Peak Forest Canal OS SK011816 Also available for corporate or private charter

The Cheese Boat

The waterways world has a reputation for being laid-back, but it is also eccentric. So when in Rome (or on the canals), it's worth going with the flow. With that in mind, don't be surprised if on an ordinary waterways day out you encounter the Cheese Boat. Geraldine and Michael Prescott live aboard their narrowboat and cruise Britain's water roads in a bid to catch the taste buds of anyone intrigued enough to sample their 'Green Thunder', 'Little Black Bomber', 'Red Devil' and other bizarre-sounding cheeses. It's a mouth-watering meeting amongst cheeses mixed with chilli, garlic, ginger, whisky and even chocolate. If you prefer not to leave the encounter to chance, track their itinerary on their website.

Details:
The Cheese Boat T:07980 871163 www.thecheeseboat.co.uk
Location:
Varies. Visit their website for details

Food for free

Nothing beats freshly picked real food. Miles of canal are bordered with hedgerows bursting with berries, nuts, flowers, herbs and seeds all year round. Hawthorn, hazel, elder are abundant. Great for jams, pies, wines.

Elderflower juice:
Grab a bunch of elder flowers fresh from the tree and throw them into a jug of boiling water. Strain when cool and serve chilled with sweetening to your taste.

Canalside Picnics

There is something Famous Fivey about a picnic with innocence, healthy natural living and everybody being nice to each other. It can't be corny to say picnics have a way of bringing out the best in us through the bond of simple food and the outdoors. You might arrive by car, parking near one of the permanent canalside picnic tables provided and get your full silver cutlery service out. Alternatively, go wild, pack a rucksack with just a water bottle, a butty and an apple and head for remoter parts. However you do it, home-prepared alfresco food tastes supreme on the waterside, just watching boats go by. The simplest things in life can be free!

Details:
For great picnic spots, find your nearest canal or why not travel to one of the 7 Wonders of the canals (see page 243), such as Caen Hill. For information on all canals, visit www.waterscape.com

Picnic on a boat

Have your picnic made for you and relax aboard the Jenny Wren on a cruise (with commentary) taking you along the Regent's Canal from Walker's Quay in the heart of London's Camden Lock to Little Venice.

Details:
Jenny Wren Canalboat Cruises T:0207 4854433 www.walkersquay.com
Location:
Walker's Quay, Camden. Regent's Canal OS TQ287840
Further info:
Preorder your picnic basket from their Waterside Restaurant, choosing from a Ploughman's Basket, Boatman's Basket and Afternoon Cream Tea Basket.

Bordeaux Quay

Slow food by the water drums with real impact at Bordeaux Quay, an old warehouse in Bristol Docks converted into Britain's first eco-gastronomic restaurant, with brasserie, wine bar, bakery, delicatessen and cookery school attached. You can tuck into simple, seasonal, deliciously cooked food and know it's so much more than eating. Here, food is about eating, cooking, shopping and learning. The place doesn't just jump onto the bandwagon of image-conscious organics: it's the real deal from 'low energy and zero waste' ethos to locally sourced ethical food. Delicious, feel good food.

Details:
Bordeaux Quay T:0117 9065550 www.bordeaux-quay.co.uk
Location:
Floating Harbour, Bristol. Kennet & Avon Canal OS ST585725

The Wheelhouse

A stylish venue with food, wine and a view of the Falkirk Wheel through the window. Little more needs to be said.

Details:
The Wheelhouse Restaurant & Bar T:01324 673490 www.wheelhousefalkirk.com
Location:
Falkirk. Forth & Clyde Canal OS NS854808
Further info:
See page 96 for their second venture, the Boathouse at Auchinstarry Marina.

Olive Press

The aroma of Italy on the canal. A former grain house with rustic beams and exposed stone, sitting in the aptly named Granary Wharf, is now a pizzeria bar and grill. Children have a chance to make their own pizza and, for every child meal sold, they donate 25p to ChildLine.

Details:
The Olive Press T:0113 2446611 www.heathcotes.co.uk/olivepress/leeds-restaurant.html
Location:
Granary Wharf, Leeds. Leeds & Liverpool Canal OS SE297330

And more...

Afloat

Feng Shang Princess: Chinese restaurant
Cumberland Basin, Regent's Canal
T:0207 4858137 www.fengshang.co.uk

Spyglass Barbecue & Grill: Converted barge
Welsh Back, Bristol. Kennet & Avon Canal
T:01179 277050 www.spyglass.org.uk

Cassoulet Barge Restaurant: Private functions
Sowerby Bridge. Rochdale Canal
T:01422 835345 www.cassoulet.co.uk

Baguette Barge: Baguettes, sandwiches, etc.
Stratford-upon-Avon. Stratford Canal
T:07963 956720 www.thebaguettebarge.com

Avon Ices - The Elizabeth: Local ice creams
Stratford-upon-Avon. Stratford Canal
T:07963 956720 www.thebaguettebarge.com

Waterside

Tipple 'n' Tiffin: Specialises in local ingredients
By theatre, Brecon Basin. Mon & Brec Canal
T:01874 611866 www.theatrbrycheiniog.co.uk

The Brasserie: Lunches, teas and ice creams
The Wharf, Bude. Bude Canal. Dog-friendly
T:01288 355275 Disabled access

Gatehouse: Modern English & Mediterranean
Lancaster. Lancaster Canal T:01524 849111
www.thegatehouserestaurant.co.uk

The Boathouse: Restaurant by the water
Near Little Venice, London. Regent's Canal
T:0207 2866752 www.boathouselondon.co.uk

Canalside: Newly refurbished bar & restaurant
Skipton. Leeds & Liverpool Canal. Local foods
T:01756 795678 www.canalsideskipton.co.uk

Teashops and cafés

Teashops are back in fashion. The doily days of self-consciously sipping tea amongst chintz and scary silence have long gone and the purifying British institution of 'a nice cup of tea' is back with Mediterranean kick. Meeting up over a cuppa or a latte has added twist on the inland waterways. Ambience, chatter and gongoozling come alfresco at stylish waterside cafés, tearooms and even floating coffee shops.

Raft Café Boat

Saunter about half an hour from historic Bath, following a scenic walk or short bike ride along the towpath, and you'll stumble upon the Raft Café, with quality Fair trade coffees and teas, panini, home-baked cakes and healthy treats. The Raft Café is a wide beam narrowboat, nonchalantly moored along the Kennet & Avon Canal on a section of towpath merrily buzzing in summer with city escapees and family bike-mania. On cooler days you can sit inside the boat on funky bar stools and let the boat stove warm you; and when the sun is sizzling you can spill out on the grassy waterside. Expect the boat to gently rock as customers arrive and leave; but don't worry about slopping your cuppa, the boat is moored securely with nifty rope work, keeping a tight hug to the canal side even when other boats ripple the water as they cruise past. A feel-good, tasty café stop, worth walking or cycling to, or even just cheat and arrive by car.

Details:
Raft Café Boat T:07733 336989
Location:
By bridge 183, Bathampton. Kennet & Avon Canal OS ST778664
What's in the area?
Bath lies in one direction, Claverton Pumping Station and John Rennie's Dundas Aqueduct in the other

@29 Coffee Shop

The old waterways world meets the new at, or should we say @, this waterside café by Grindley Brook staircase locks. Great watering hole and food stop for boaters or anyone passing on the towpath, as well as a perfect gongoozler spot. The clue in its name is that it's an internet cafe too. Gifts and canal souvenirs add spice to the coffee and cake.

Details:
@29 Coffee Shop T:01948 663385
Location:
By Grindley Brook staircase locks, Grindley Brook. Llangollen Canal OS SJ523430
What's in the area?
Great walking country: the South Cheshire Way, Bishop Bennet Way, Maelor Way, Shropshire Way, Marches Way and Sandstone Trail all meet here

Hatton Locks Café

The Grand Union Canal which links London and the Midlands once transported working narrowboats laden with cargoes of spices, sugars and teas. Boats travel lighter these days, for fun – and you get tea served on the canal side instead. Hatton Locks Café is a great place to soak up a sunny afternoon, watching boats pass. 21 locks raise the Grand Union Canal from the Avon valley, and it's not hard to see how Hatton Locks got the nickname 'Stairway to Heaven'. History bursts from every bridge, bend, lock gate and plaque. Even the cafe tells its tale of a former life stabling boat horses with tethering rings and a drainage channel for horses' doings visible through a glass display panel. A good selection of light snacks is offered with the added interest of canal gifts. For kids there are grassy spaces to romp and explore interactive educational installations tastefully planted along the lock flight.

Details:
Hatton Locks Café T:01926 409432
Location:
By Hatton Top Lock, Hatton. Grand Union Canal OS SP242668
What's in the area?
Explore the locks, take brass rubbings along the flight, or visit Warwick

Canalside Café

The aptly named café tucks tightly on the canal side overlooking historic Gas Street Basin. Once the lock keeper's cottage, it's now a rustic, no fuss place that's a quirky pub-café-restaurant all rolled into one. Beefy folk won't even notice it's a veggie haven. A relaxed city hang-out for a waterside drink.

Details:
Canalside Café T:0121 2487979 Vegetarian
Location:
At Worcester Bar, Birmingham. Birmingham Canal Navigations OS SP062865
What's in the area?
The Mailbox, Brindley Place, National Indoor Arena & National Sealife Centre (see page 195)

Floating Coffee Company

If you're visiting Birmingham, the capital of the canals, look out for the Floating Coffee Company in Brindley Place. A traditional narrowboat named George is permanently moored at the heart of bustling Birmingham in the up-market waterways zone. Hop aboard for a moment of peace and a retreat from the hubbub. Espresso, cappuccino, latte, it's got the lot, and serves hearty food all day too. You might have to be patient to get a seat, but who's in a hurry on the waterways - even in the city? The interior is compact and traditional, with its galley-kitchen in the bow. The crew-staff are huggably friendly.

Details:
'George', Floating Coffee Company T:0121 6330050 www.sherbornewharf.co.uk
Location:
At Brindley Place, Birmingham. Birmingham Canal Navigations OS SP060867
What's in the area?
You're in the centre of Brindley Place (see page 195), with shopping and culture all around!

Caen Hill Café

There's no enforced way to arrive at Caen Hill Café. Come by bike, boat or boot and it beckons like a gingerbread house from leafiness at the summit of Caen Hill Locks. The café itself is pleasantly unassuming and basic, but the point of being here isn't really the tea and cake – it's sitting out on the terrace overlooking the lock flight.

Details:
Caen Hill Café T:01380 724880
Location:
By lock 44, Devizes. Kennet & Avon Canal SO ST988615
What's in the area?
Caen Hill Locks, one of the 7 wonders of the waterways (see page 243)

Devon cream tea

A cream tea is the great British experience; but a floating cream tea on Devon's own waters is special. Expect more than a quick cuppa with the ducks when you climb aboard the Ducks' Ditty, a barge café-bar moored at Tiverton Wharf on the Grand Western Canal. A Tivertonian Cream Tea is to drool for: 'One freshly baked Scone, halved and topped with Clotted Cream and Strawberry Jam, with a wedge of home-baked Sponge Cake and a cup of tea.' Somehow the mock 19th-century boaty costumes the staff wear manage not to stoop into twee since there's enough evocative distraction from the horse-drawn boat trips and old-fashioned canalia (canal crafts and souvenirs) shop just along the towpath.

Details:
Ducks' Ditty Floating Café Bar T:01884 253345 www.tivertoncanal.co.uk
Location:
At Tiverton Wharf, Tiverton. Grand Western Canal OS SS963123
What's in the area?
The entire canal is a natural park and there are horse-drawn boat rides (see page 35) and rowing boat hire from the wharf

Moonraker Floating Tearoom

A narrowboat permanently moored in historic Slaithwaite (pronounced 'slawit' by locals) village, surrounded by woollen mills, northern charisma and tales of bygone smugglers (time your visit with the Moonraking festival in February - see page 118). Slaithwaite is the only village in England with a canal running alongside its main street. Fresh homemade breakfasts, cakes and lunches.

Details:
Moonraker Floating Tearoom T:01484 846370
Location:
By Dartmouth Lock 23E, Slaithwaite. Huddersfield Narrow Canal OS SE077138
What's in the area?
A short towpath walk through the Colne Valley to Marsden and the Standedge Tunnel, one of the 7 wonders of the waterways (see page 243)

THE FLOATING COFFEE Co.

BRINDLEYPLACE
Tel 0121 633 0050

505487

MOONRAKER

FLOATING TEAROOM

PROP. VAL TODD SLAITHWAITE

And more...

Afloat

The Coffee Boat: T:07815 138912
Bradford on Avon. Kennet & Avon Canal
Converted working boat near the Tithe Barn

Gongoozler's Rest Café: T:07730 125849
Braunston. Grand Union Canal
Narrowboat moored by the Marina

Waterside

Canal Tea Room: T:01506 671215
Linlithgow Canal Centre. Union Canal
Centre hosts the Scottish Canal Museum

Waterside Café: T:020 72661066
Little Venice, London. Regent's Canal
Sit inside or out in the heart of Little Venice

Waterside Rest: T:01873 881069
Goytre Wharf. Mon & Brec Canal
In the historic setting of Goytre Wharf

Tea Room & Gift shop: T:01978 860702
Llangollen Wharf. Llangollen Canal
Horse-drawn boat trips set off from here

Crinan Coffee Shop: T:01546 830261
Lochgilphead. Crinan Canal
Part of Crinan Hotel in stunning scenery

Fradley Canalside Café: T:01827 252000
Fradley Junction. Coventry Canal
Gongoozlers' heaven in midst of lock flight

Waterside Café: T:01270 626171
Nantwich. Shropshire Union Canal
Award-winning café in Canal Centre

Five Rise Locks Café: T:01274 562221
Bingley. Leeds & Liverpool Canal
Viewpoint by Five Rise Locks (see page 243)

Go to the pub

It's a very British thing. Waterside inns somehow have the extra canny knack of getting you to chill out with a full glass in your hand and no thoughts of rushing off. Pubs have been part of canal culture since the beginning when navvies spent their days digging the cut and their nights soothed by song and ale. The toil of the canal builders and working boatmen spices the character of many ancient waterside inns, often with relics of the past remaining and raunchy tales the locals like to tell. Luckily, revolting giant theme-chain pubs and tasteless beer don't always get their brutish way along the canals. Local real ale and a real welcome are a tradition canals won't give up without a fight. Nothing beats toasting your toes in winter beside a roaring log fire with the warm afterglow of a golden boatman's ale. In summer a lazy afternoon is best spent in the beer garden gongoozling (watching the water world travel by) while you sip locally brewed cider and chat. Take time in life for moments like this.

Tunnel End Inn

Marsden is a northern mill town on the Huddersfield Narrow Canal near the famous Standedge Tunnel. The locals are at first glance as ordinary as anyone, but old legends lie on their tongues and given half a chance they'll turn anything into a festival. Scattered through the seasons you can expect Morris dancers swilling ale between leaps, and funky happenings at events such as the Imbolc, Cuckoo Day and Marsden Jazz Festival (see page 116). Of course, at the heart of any festival there usually lies a good pub: the Tunnel End Inn, by no coincidence, manages to be involved in most festival shenanigans around these parts. You can party all day, then tuck into meat and tatty pie washed down with a pint of real ale. If the charms of this CAMRA pub get the better of you and you fancy staying over for a full day's sightseeing tomorrow, book into the self-contained apartment adjoined to the inn. It sleeps from just one person, to a family or small group and offers the flexibility of coming and going as you please with a separate entrance from the pub. Marsden snuggles on the northern boundary of the Peak District National Park, so at quiet times between festivals you can walk in peace across the moors or take a gentler stroll along the canal. The Tunnel End Inn offers a warm welcome all year round, with roaring fires in winter and sizzling views in summer. Oozing West Yorkshire charm.

Details:
Tunnel End Inn T:01484 844636 www.tunnelendinn.com
Location:
Marsden, West Yorkshire. Huddersfield Narrow Canal OS SE040121
What's in the area?
It's just up the road from the Standedge Tunnel, one of the 7 wonders of the waterways (see page 243), and its Visitor Centre
Further info:
Marsden Moor Exhibition Centre, National Trust Estate Office, Marsden T:01484 847016
Offers information on walks, events and the area

The Boathouse

The Boathouse at Auchinstarry Marina on the Forth & Clyde Canal is only 10 miles from one of Scotland's most visited attractions, the Falkirk Wheel. It is Scotland's first specially designed eco-friendly pub and was built in partnership with British Waterways using sustainable timber, with geothermal heating and reed bed waste treatments. In a picturesque setting, overlooking the water with the Campsie Fells in the background, you wouldn't have a clue that Glasgow stomps around the corner. You're invited to sink into a chair, watch boats on the water, enjoy the sensory garden or explore the nature trail. The hospitality is Scottish, warm and unpretentious. Good food is served all day, every day. If you decide to stay, there are ten 4-star luxurious bedrooms where you can sleep with the lullaby of water and silence. It's a place to slow down and get dreamy about sailing into the sunset on a romantic barge.

Details:
The Boathouse T:01236 829200 www.boathousekilsyth.com
Location:
Auchinstarry Marina, Kilsyth. Forth & Clyde Canal OS NS720768
What's in the area?
The marina, canal and boats, and a short drive from the Falkirk Wheel (see page 243)

Star Inn

Stone calls itself a canal town and the Star Inn, perched on the lock side, predates the canal by about a century. There's usually plenty to watch if you sit outside or grab a window seat inside overlooking the lock. Beware of the low beams and intoxicatingly uneven stone floors: Guinness World Records lists the pub for having more levels than any other English pub.

Details:
The Star Inn T:01785 813096 Dogs allowed in the Tap room
Location:
By lock 27, Stone. Trent & Mersey Canal OS SJ902336
What's in the area?
The busy high street is a short walk away, and the oldest hire operator on the canals, Canal Cruising Company, is based in the nearby boatyard. www.canalcruising.co.uk

The Apple

The Apple is a converted Dutch barge moored in Bristol's floating harbour. With a quayside terrace and on-board bar, here is the place to chill with exceptionally cool cider. Famous for its 'Old Bristolian Cider', at 8.4% proof it's only served in half-pint glasses for a lethal night out. Locally it's known by city workers and as a student hang-out, but its chilled culture attracts visitors from afar – young, old, those spiked with alternative attitude or cool conservatism. Around 40 different ciders are on offer with bizarre concoctions from raspberry cider to cider cocktails. If cider is like Marmite to you, there are also beers and wines, as well as curiously named platters of good food. It's friendly and buzzing with waterside atmosphere.

Details:
The Apple T:0117 9253500 www.applecider.co.uk
Location:
Welsh Back, Bristol. Kennet & Avon Canal OS ST589726
What's in the area?
Bristol's Floating Harbour and quayside with boats and ships including the SS Great Britain

Camden cool

Lock 17 is a trendy bar at the happening heart of London's Camden. Pop in after a day's shopping in the famous markets or arrive at night for live music and a different ambience. The experience seems to change depending on the time of day, day of the week (and probably the direction of the wind) from just chilling out in the Canalside or Terrace Bars with their fab views over Regent's Canal to the more hyped buzz of shoulder bumping and cocktail swilling with drunken intent. This chameleon never loses its Camden cool though.

Details:
Lock 17 T:0207 4285929 www.lock17-camden.co.uk
Location:
By Camden Lock, London. Regent's Canal OS TQ286841
What's in the area?
Camden is renowned for its markets and trendy shops, and there's the added interest of watching boats go through the double locks. Visit www.camdenlock.net for more info.

The George

Full of Olde English cosiness. A character-packed pub with exposed beams, real fires, nooks, crannies and cubbyhole-sized rooms to snuggle up and forget the world. The 12th-century building was once a monastery and, for ultra authenticity, conceals a traditional priest-hole. The pub can brag about its Cask Marque Accreditation, but if beer isn't your thing (although if you taste a pint here it may well become your thing) try their wines, coffees or herbal teas hospitably served. Olive fans can tuck in at the bar, and the food menu is seriously appetizing. In summer the charisma spreads outside with alfresco gongoozling casually straddling the towpath. Only a walk or bike ride from Bath, this stretch of the Kennet & Avon Canal is popular (see page 63). The pub welcomes children, but doesn't stoop to tacky 'family fun' elements ruining it for grown ups. A pub with a waterside view, and just about everything else that matters.

Details:
George Inn T:01225 425079 www.thespiritgroup.com
Location:
By bridge 183, Bathampton. Kennet & Avon Canal OS ST776664
What's in the area?
Short towpath walk or ride to Bath in one direction, Dundas Aqueduct in the other
Further info:
Dogs allowed in outdoor areas only. Good wheelchair access with designated loos and car parking.

CAMRA

The Campaign for Real Ale (CAMRA) is a voluntary organisation campaigning for quality real ale, real pubs and consumer rights. With over 95,000 members, CAMRA promotes high standards within the industry through its Pub of the Year and Champion Beer of Britain awards. CAMRA organises local and national fundraising beer festivals throughout the year all over the UK.

Details:
Campaign for Real Ale T:01727 867201 www.camra.org.uk

And more...

Bridge Inn: T:01380 860273
By Horton Bridge (134), Kennet & Avon Canal
Listed as one of top 10 waterside pubs in UK

Dusty Miller: www.dustymiller-wrenbury.com
Characterful converted mill by Wrenbury Lift
Bridge, Llangollen Canal T:01270 780537

Eagle Barge Pub: A converted Dutch barge
Laggan Locks, Caledonian Canal
T:07789 858567 www.theeaglebarge.com

Swan Inn: T:01283 790330
Fradley Junction. Trent & Mersey Canal
Great for gongoozling in picturesque location

Shroppie Fly: A boat forms part of the bar
The Wharf, Audlem. Shropshire Union Canal
T:01270 811772 www.shroppiefly.co.uk

The Water Witch: Converted canalside stables
Between bridges 98 & 99, Lancaster Canal
www.thewaterwitch.co.uk T:01524 63828

Anchor Inn: T:01785 284569
High Offley. Shropshire Union Canal
Traditional unspoilt pub with campsite

The Weighbridge: CAMRA award-winning pub
Alvechurch. Worcester & Birmingham Canal
T:0121 4455111 www.the-weighbridge.co.uk

The Turf: T:01392 833128 www.turfpub.net
By Turf Lock, Exeter Ship Canal
Local food/ales. No cars: only boat, bike, boot!

Navigation Inn: Overlooking historic Bugsworth
Basin, Buxworth. Peak Forest Canal.
www.navigationinn.co.uk T:01663 732072

More pubs on www.coolcanalsguides.com

Living history

17th-century eyebrows raised at the new canals' revolutionary engineering, but no one could have imagined how much would remain in operation for us today, without need of change (and still eyebrows raise!). Canals changed Britain's landscape and fortunes over 200 years ago in the name of the Industrial Revolution: but the rumbling of grimy industrialisation is mostly a romantic memory whispering across the waterways today. Traditional narrowboats, the folk art of Roses and Castles, iconic landmarks, old-fashioned camaraderie and stories that still travel by word of mouth keep waterways history fresh and deliciously alive. This isn't stuffy indoor history, it lives on to tell its own story to anyone who cares to join in. All you have to do is take a walk, climb aboard a narrowboat, or simply drop into an ancient canalside pub.

NOTICE.
This
BRIDGE
Is insufficient to carry a
HEAVY MOTOR CAR
The Registered Axle Weight of any axle of which exceeds
TONS
or the Registered Axle-Weights of the several
Axles of which exceed in the aggregate
TONS
or a Heavy Motor Car drawing a
TRAILER
if the Registered Axle-Weights of the several Axles
of the HEAVY MOTOR CAR and the
Axle-Weights of the several Axles of the
TRAILER
Exceed in the aggregate

GREAT WESTERN RAILWAY CO
PADDINGTON STATION
LONDON

Roses and Castles

It's doubtful that the stiff canal-building entrepreneurs and bankers of the Industrial Revolution could have imagined the romantic canal culture of art and creativity born from their more vulgar motives. The spirit of art flows through canal life. Everywhere you look the traditional canal folk art of crudely daubed Roses and Castles decorates pots and pans, narrowboats' doors and kitsch trinkets in canalside stores. Ordinary working boat people (who would not have thought of themselves as artists) originally created the theme of Roses and Castles over 2 centuries ago. Almost with a mania, they decorated any surface they could on their boat, and all its paraphernalia. The interior of the boatman's cabin, water cans, poles, door panels, even the nose bowl for the horse that pulled the boat, all sparkled with the characteristic decoration of Roses and Castles. Working boat families lived in cramped conditions so everything had to be functional. Perhaps that's one reason decoration was so elaborately applied in every crevice. No one really knows why the theme was adopted, but we like to think that Roses and Castles were the narrowboat families' way of cushioning the harsh struggle of their confined living conditions, and perhaps their home was a castle, and their garden was always full of roses!

Waterways Craft Guild

Aims to maintain the high standards of traditional skills of waterways' arts and crafts. Membership for painters of narrowboats, giftware, roses & castles, also signwriters and makers of fenders, ropework, crochet work and cabin lace. They run courses in most traditional crafts at locations throughout the UK, with details on their website.

Details:
Waterways Craft Guild www.waterwayscraftguild.org.uk

Guild of Waterway Artists

Formed to accredit and promote commercial art. Their website lists members of the Guild and exhibitions of their art around the country.

Details:
Guild of Waterway Artists www.waterwayartists.org.uk

Black Country Living Museum

Canals themselves are only half a story; the industries that they were built for is the other. An area in the Midlands, aptly nicknamed The Black Country, grew up in the boom years of the Industrial Revolution manufacturing chains, ships' anchors, nails, locks and keys. Significantly for the workforce, the Black Country is also renowned for its breweries and boasts more pubs per mile than almost anywhere in Britain. The canal networks are dense in the Midlands with reminders of urban heritage along many water miles. For an authentic experience of yesteryear, visit the 26-acre Black Country Museum. The region's historic buildings were saved from demolition and rebuilt brick by brick at the museum site creating an urban canalside village. Staff dress in costume and craftsmen demonstrate Black Country skills. There's plenty to do and see: shop in the traditional sweet shop, take a lesson in an old-fashioned school, see the underground coal mine, visit exhibition halls, see limestone caverns and explore much more. The whole package sounds a bit bizarre, yet manages never to stoop into crass tourism. Black Country humour and a traditional bag of fish and chips with mushy peas, swilled down by a pint of the Black Country's best mild ale will make the day.

Details:
Black Country Living Museum T:0121 5579643 www.bclm.org.uk Some disabled access
Location:
Dudley. Birmingham Canal Navigations OS SO950915
Further info:
Open every day March to October, rest of year closed Mon-Tues

Singing cavern

Throw caution to the wind in the Singing Cavern. Concerts inside a tunnel are an acoustic sensation. The cavern branches off the Dudley Tunnel and can only be reached by boat. To add to the drama, poor ventilation means all craft must be electric powered or legged through the tunnel. Dudley Canal Trust runs year-round events such as live jazz and even orchestral concerts in the tunnel.

Details:
Dudley Canal Trust T:01384 236275 www.dudleycanaltrust.org.uk

Red House Glass Cone

Stourbridge was once world renowned for its glassmaking and the Red House Glass Cone still beckons from the skyline like a cathedral of the glass industry. Outside it's powerful and beautiful. Inside, the spirit of its past makes for an intense experience. Stourbridge Cone is one of only 4 still standing in Britain and the best preserved across Europe. It ceased production in 1936 and is now a visitors' centre offering glass-making demonstrations, displays of historic tools, audio and visual exhibitions, a shop and a canalside café evocatively on the spot where narrowboats once loaded cargo from the Cone. 21st-century intrusions don't spoil the quintessential experience though, and the ferocity of yesteryear's furnace still burns the imagination. From the dark sweaty centre of the Cone, the eye is pulled upwards to concentric brick circles in a tunnel to the sky. At its end a dot of light pierces the void as if in remembrance of smog from burning coal that would have bellowed into the harsh working class atmosphere that gave the area its name. In contrast to the industrial darkness and heat inside the Cone, the adjacent shop and Stuart Crystal Gift Centre ironically sparkle delicately with light and shelves of fine glass artefacts. Purchases are not obligatory, but they are hard to resist.

Details:
Red House Glass Cone T:01384 812750 www.dudley.gov.uk FREE admission. Disabled access
Location:
By Glasshouse Bridge, Wordsley, Stourbridge. Stourbridge Canal OS SO894864
Further info:
Open all year except Christmas
Don't miss:
The glass sculpture by Robyn Smith and Robert Foxall that won the prize for Creative Spacial response in 2006. A lace curtain finely created in glass catches an imaginary breeze and glimpse of light from a tiny window inside the cone walls. It's an impressive installation of art that subtly tells the story of working conditions, the intensity of the furnace and the sheer beauty of light and glass. In its context it makes a stunningly powerful work of art.

A day in the docks

Don't fool yourself that you can visit and rush off before lunch. Make a day of it. Wandering around Gloucester's historic docks gives a real sense of its former life and the hubbub of its formidable past. These docks have been part of shipping history since Roman times and, as Britain's most inland port, in its heyday tall ships would have ridden the infamous tides of the River Severn to join long queues along the canal waiting to unload cargos of grain and timber. Uniform cubes of elegantly restored Victorian warehouses stand bold and beautiful, patterned by bricks of a past century's colours. Everywhere you look original features milk the atmosphere: rail tracks, mooring rings, signposts and a steam crane. A church in its midst secludes maritime blessings and salvation for drunken boatmen. History is satisfying as the whole place clinks with the presence of today. Any summer day paints a scene of ducks, swans, water, people messing with their boats, and swing bridges that lift, stopping the city's traffic for daily boat trips. In spring and winter, restaurants waft aromas of calamares and garlic to mix in the outdoor air with wood from the narrowboaters' stoves. The museum at Gloucester Docks is housed inside Llanthony Warehouse. Touchscreen displays, working models, interactive displays and a diary of events and special activities make this museum a must. It's refreshingly not one of those places where you have to keep nagging the kids 'not to touch'. You can even step inside a traditional working narrowboat to appreciate at first hand living conditions for boat families. For a grand day out, take a picnic or try one of the waterside bars.

Details:
National Waterways Museum T:01452 318200 www.nwm.org.uk/gloucester Disabled access
Location:
The Docks, Gloucester. Gloucester & Sharpness Canal OS SO827183
Further info:
The National Waterways Museum is one museum on three sites, Ellesmere Port, Stoke Bruerne and Gloucester Docks, with different displays and historic boats at each.
Don't miss:
Even if you don't like antiques, the antique shop in the docks is worth a visit. Don't be put off by the understated frontage. Floors of intrigue await inside with everything from 1960s Dandy comics to that life-sized brass lion you've been looking for.

And more...

The life of working boat horses:

Some signs from the past were never intentionally made, yet give descending generations a visible taste of the raw truth of working life on the cut. Scrutinize the underside of bridges, and on some you will see deep rope-burned gouges from horses tugging narrowboats laden with cargo. After a gruelling day hauling the boat, a working horse's day often ended in basic stabling at a canalside inn. Some inns even leave clues of the stabling from yesteryear.

Details:
The Horseboating Society aims to promote horseboating and preserve its heritage and skills. Membership and training.
www.horseboating.org.uk

Weavers' Triangle Trust

Preserving Burnley's textile heritage & one of the finest surviving Victorian industrial landscapes in the country.

Details:
Visitor Centre. Leeds & Liverpool Canal
T:01282 452403 www.weaverstriangle.co.uk

Crofton Pumping Station

Grade I-listed building containing the oldest working beam engine in the world. Tea room.

Details:
T:01672 870300 www.croftonbeamengines.org

London Canal Museum

London. Regent's Canal Disabled access

Details:
T:0207 7130836 www.canalmuseum.org.uk

Festivals

The spirit of festival is at the heart of the waterways. Any excuse will do for a waterside party. The traditional, the quirky and the downright eccentric. And it's not just about boats and water. As you'd expect from any good fest, there's usually ice cream, veggie burgers, the aroma of coffee beans and of course the indomitable beer tent or strategically nearby real ale pub. But what makes a waterways party ultra special is chilled chatter from distinctly laid-back canal culture. It's a gathering on land and water where narrowboaters are armed with Brasso for bouts of one-upmanship in stem to stern rivalry. After you've peered into every boat and perhaps been on a boat trip, you might have time to wander around some stalls and buy anything from a badge or a boaty hat to a painting or a pot decorated in canal art. There's always space for kids to be kids and it all boils down to a full day's entertainment with something for almost everyone. A lot of wandering around and utterly harmless loitering. Wear comfy shoes!

Middlewich Folk and Boat Festival

Sumptuous, wholesome folkie fun for all the family. A weekend of music, water, boats and good cheap canalside camping for the complete festival deal. Traditional narrowboat crafts, street performers, dance, workshops and lots of fringe events are on offer.

Details:
Middlewich Folk & Boat Festival T:0709 2390501 www.midfest.org.uk Held in mid June
Location:
Middlewich, Cheshire. Trent & Mersey Canal OS SJ704661

Crinan Classic

Scotland at its rugged best. On the wild Atlantic side, the fishing village of Crinan hosts fierce boat racing, haggis hurling, boat tug-a-war, Ceilidhs and whisky swilling. Bring a wooden boat with you if you have one. Sailing boats, motorboats and dinghies to fishing boats - anything fits in, as long as it's wooden. Don't go expecting formalities, the fun is ferocious.

Details:
Crinan Classic Boat Festival T:01546 830261 www.crinanclassic.com Held at the beginning of July
Location:
Crinan. Crinan Canal OS NR790943

IWA Canalway Cavalcade

That certain town in Italy may yet rank down to 'Little London' for one day each year when London's Little Venice hosts its big water event. Usually over 100 boats gather with pageants of decorated boats, illuminated processions on the water, boat-handling activities, boat trips, trade stalls, music, theatre and always plenty to interest the kids.

Details:
Inland Waterways' Association Canalway Cavalcade T:01494 783453 www.waterways.org.uk Held on Bank Holiday weekend beginning of May
Location:
Little Venice, London. Regent's Canal OS TQ262818

Rake the moon from the canal

Wrap up warm, follow the crowd and go moonraking along the Huddersfield Narrow Canal. A festival pumped with quirky canal history. Every February, the villagers of Slaithwaite come together (with a hearty bunch of outsiders gatecrashing) to bring back to life the dastardly story of two Slaithwaite rogues. The tale goes that, one frosty day in 1802, the said duo were smuggling barrels of liquor from a boat when patrolling soldiers disturbed them. The rogues hid the barrels in reeds and returned later under the cover of darkness. Soldiers again disturbed them, but the quick-witted rogues yelled, "Cans tha noon seah? T'mooin fell int watter an we'ar rekkin er aht!". The soldiers went off sniggering at the duo's stupidity. The smugglers' triumph is a nifty excuse for a weekend of carnival over two centuries on. Lanterns float down the canal, toe-tapping music rings in the air and of course the giant Mr Moon makes his appearance. Big on atmosphere with a mighty dose of British eccentricity.

Details:
Moonraking Festival www.slaithwaitemoonraking.org Held during February Half Term
Location:
Slaithwaite, West Yorks. Huddersfield Narrow Canal OS SE079139

Imbolc Fire Festival

Something in the Pennine air keeps old legends alive and, for the locals of Marsden, one story has become an annual tradition with all sorts of canalside shenanigans. Every year the town hosts the battle between Jack Frost (winter) and Mr Green (spring) as they come to loggerheads over the passing seasons. A procession from Standedge Visitor Centre to the Tunnel End Inn ends in the battle. Luckily the inn serves real ale and home-cooked food so the hearty celebrations can last as long as it takes.

Details:
Imbolc Fire Festival www.kirkless.gov.uk Held in early February
Location:
Marsden, West Yorkshire. Huddersfield Narrow Canal OS SE040120

Sowerby Rushbearing Festival

A bunch of around 60 men making their way to the pub could sound thuggish, but not when they are dressed in Panama hats and wearing clogs. This funky festival has deceptively practical roots. Centuries ago rushes were used to cover church floors and, once a year, carts of new rushes would be brought to replace the old. Yorkshire spirit typically celebrated the event with music, merriment and Morris men. Today it's evolved into a weekend of clog-clonking fun. A 16-foot high two-wheeled rush cart, lavishly adorned, is pulled in a procession by 60 local men dressed for the part, whilst the lucky women get to ride precariously on the cart. A few token rushes get dropped off at the churches, but the mission is to end up at the canal basin, with liquid entertainment in mind.

Details:
Rushbearing Festival www.rushbearing.co.uk Held in early September
Location:
Sowerby Bridge, West Yorkshire. Rochdale Canal OS SE066236

Marsden Cuckoo Day

Marsden's ancient legend goes that when the cuckoo arrived he brought springtime, sunshine and hope. In a bid to keep hold of springtime forever Marsden's folk of yore built a tower around the cuckoo. Churlishly all didn't go to plan. "It were nobbut just wun course too low" the legend says. If one more layer had been built, it might have worked but the bird flew away of course! The idea of keeping sunshine in the tower might be completely barmy but given the Pennine reputation for rain, the desire is faultless. Today Marsden people drag out the clogs for a daylong festival of music and dance, with drinks and fun after the procession and 'cuckoo walk' to celebrate the return of the cuckoo.

Details:
Marsden Cuckoo Day www.bellastown.demon.co.uk Held in late April
Location:
Marsden, West Yorkshire. Huddersfield Narrow Canal OS SE048117

Crick Boat Show

Every May, a sleepy picturesque corner of Northamptonshire bursts at the seams with festival fever. Crick Marina on the Grand Union Canal becomes the outdoor venue for a much-coveted waterways event that's infamous amongst boaters. Hundreds of boats line the water, from canoes to wide beam boats, but narrowboats are always the stars of this show. This is your chance to wander through dizzy numbers of spanking new narrowboats and dream (or scheme) to buy. There's plenty of stuff to do from free boat trips to boot-stomping music with hundreds of stalls heaving with anything from the latest boat paraphernalia to the obligatory festival fudge, as well as finger food and the happy beer tent. Kids get storytelling, craft workshops and plenty of grassy space to do what kids do. Britain being Britain, rain has been known to blight the event, some years with mud swamps to rival Glastonbury's worst. Other years have seen picnickers melting with strawberries and cream on sun-toasted grass. But whatever the weather, the tradition is stalwart good humour.

Details:
Crick Boat Show T:0871 7000685 www.crickboatshow.com Held on Bank Holiday end of May
Location:
Crick, Northants. Grand Union Canal OS SP595726

IWA National Festival

Every year gazebos and flags air their creases when they come out for the IWA National Festival. It's the waterways event of the year. All in the good cause of fundraising for the canals, it's the one not to miss. Expect boats, stalls, food and drink, events and activities. Held in a different place along the networks every year, the locality's accent guarantees to infuse the event.

Details:
IWA National Festival T:01494 783453 www.waterways.org.uk Location varies each year
Further info:
Held on Bank Holiday end of August. Inland Waterways' Association 'Campaigning for the use, maintenance and restoration of Britain's inland waterways'

And more...

Norbury Junction Canal Festival: May
Norbury Junction. Shropshire Union Canal
www.sncanal.org.uk

Skipton Waterway Festival: May
Skipton. Leeds & Liverpool Canal
www.penninecruisers.com T:01756 795478

IWA National Trailboat Festival: May
Location varies each year
www.waterways.org.uk T:01494 783453

Etruria Canals Festival: May
Stoke-on-Trent. Trent & Mersey Canal
T:01782 233144

Historic Narrowboat Rally & Canal Festival:
June. Braunston. Grand Union Canal
www.braunstonmarina.co.uk T:01788 891373

Audlem Music & Art Festival: May
Audlem. Shropshire Union Canal
www.audlemfestival.com T:07813 820157

Newbury Waterways Festival: July
Newbury. Kennet & Avon Canal
www.katrust.org

Kirkintilloch Canal Festival: August
Kirkintilloch. Forth & Clyde Canal
www.kirkintillochcanalfestival.org.uk

Saltaire Festival: September
Saltaire. Leeds & Liverpool Canal
www.saltairefestival.co.uk

Dudley Festival of Water & Light: October
Waterfront, Merry Hill. Dudley No.1 Canal
www.dudley.gov.uk

More festivals on www.coolcanalsguides.com

Kids' stuff

You've told them you're taking them somewhere special, and the next thing you know, they're experiencing the wide-eyed freedom of a forgotten world, totally new to them. A very special place to grow, breath, explore. Back in the industrial heyday of the canals, kids were merely cheap labour; luckily today's waterways are an open-air adventure with endless ways for kids to be creative and play in safety. Somewhere to enjoy cultural fun, lap up the great outdoors and revel in the responsibility of being together as a family, without the tedium of plastic or electronic entertainment. Children are always fascinated by canals, but if you spark their imagination before a visit, the excitement grows. Bake duck-shaped biscuits, paint Roses and Castles, make a traditional boatman's bandana for the dog, learn about different boats, make a pictionary of canal words, collect a wildlife file and see how many songs the kids can think of related to water and boats.

Bike rides, waterside camping, festivals - of course every page in this guide is bursting with stuff for kids to do, but this chapter is for kids only!

Just go for a walk

Free, healthy, good old-fashioned fun for kids. It sounds obvious, but it's easy to forget or underestimate the simple pleasures children get from healthy walks. And walking in the waterways world can be like entering a wonderland with the fertile playground of your children's minds. There's so much to see, do, sense, explore, and you'll get all the sparkle of seeing canals through their eyes. Older kids get a buzz out of 'how many miles can I walk in a day?' rising to the A to B challenge, while younger children will focus better with staged points of interest to explore as they walk.

Cool things for younger kids to carry:

Younger children love the sense of ownership that packing their own bag brings. Don't be fooled by them though, you know whatever they pack into their rucksacks, you'll end up carrying eventually! Steer with steely subtlety so that big Ted stays home and little Ted gets to come.

On the walk:

Allow time to stop off and explore.
Plan plenty of snack breaks.
Set the pace with the youngest legs in mind.
Don't be afraid to change the day's itinerary if it seems over ambitious.
If the kids have made their own map of the route before the walk, they'll love leading the way and pointing out landmarks of interest.
Vary the walk by mixing up the pace, taking turns to lead or hop on a narrowboat for part of the way (boats can be hired for the day, or part of the day, and there are plenty of organised boat trips (see pages 37-38).
Collect things along the way - photos, drawings, diary notes, new words.
Don't forget kids' walks can include wheels – buggies and bikes are cool.

Further info:
For details on every canal in the network, visit www.waterscape.com

Somerset Space Walk

This is where the waterways world meets the universe. Kids can explore the planets in our solar system simply by going for a walk along the canal. The Bridgewater & Taunton Canal is scattered with sculptures of the planets mathematically positioned, in true scale, on the canal side. Start at the Sun by Higher Maunsel Lock, and follow the 6-mile trail either way (the orbit centres around the sun). Whichever direction you choose, you can pop into a pub just before Pluto.

Details:
Somerset Space Walk T:01452 318000 Maunsel Canal Centre T:01823 663160
Location:
Higher Maunsel Lock, Bridgwater & Taunton Canal OS ST308294
Further info:
The walk was the brainchild of Pip Youngman and was officially opened in August 1997 by British astronomer Heather Crouper. Teas at Maunsel Lock Tea Garden & Canal Centre. Boat trips are also available from here.

Visit a different London

Don't visit the queen, or do the usual touristy stuff: explore London's backwaters instead. Make a day of it by catching the waterbus from Little Venice to Camden Lock, keeping your eyes open for non-native creatures along the way as the canal cuts through London Zoo (entrance via their own canal gate can be included). Visit London's Canal Museum, then wind up the perfect day with a floating Chinese on the Feng Shang Princess, or a meal at the Boathouse restaurant. No trip to the city is complete without going to the theatre, and it's extra fun when it's a puppet theatre on a barge. The Puppet Barge is a floating theatre moored in Little Venice during winter and spring, and travelling the Thames in the summer months for audiences at Henley, Marlow, Cliveden and Richmond-on-Thames.

Details:
Puppet Barge T:0207 2496876 www.puppetbarge.com Location varies. Access difficult for wheelchairs. The auditorium has a hearing loop. Seats 50. See their website for latest info.
Further info:
London Waterbus (see page 41), London Canal Museum (see page 111), Feng Shang Princess and The Boathouse restaurant (see page 79)

Spooky appointment

Stories handed down say that navvies and 18th-century boatmen may have been scared of ghoulish happenings on misty canal waters. But tales of cackling white ladies and spooky moans from deep inside dripping canal tunnels don't scare this millennium's kids or grown-ups, do they? Tunnels are reputedly the favourite hang-outs for ghosts. Poor old Kit Crewbucket was murdered, and her headless corpse dumped inside the Harecastle Tunnel on the Trent & Mersey Canal. It's said she's haunted the gloomy place ever since. Scarcely a canal across the land misses the chance to run spooky Halloween trips, claiming fame for a local ghost or two.

Further info:
To find a Halloween tunnel boat trip near you, visit www.waterscape.com

Santa boat trips

Nothing travels at speed on the waterways - except Santa! As Christmas draws near, Mr Claus takes to his narrowboat tiller and manages a magical appearance with his floating grotto on a canal in almost every corner of the land. Sackfuls of waterways festivity.

Further info:
For Santa boat trips around the country, visit www.coolcanalsguides.com

Duck race

Take the kids or just unleash yourself, and join in the duck race. Hundreds of yellow ducks bob on the water with plastic attitude. Each has a number, and you make your pledge to your chosen duck. The race is on and, shoulder to shoulder, the crowd jumps up and down along the canal banks cheering allegiances. It's vicious fun.

Further info:
For a list of duck races around the country, see www.coolcanalsguides.com

And more...

WOW

'Learning is fun' is a term that tends to be bandied about willy-nilly these days but WOW genuinely comes up with the goods. Wild over Waterways is a partnership between British Waterways, the Waterways Trust and the Inland Waterways' Association bringing loads of great resources together for kids, parents and teachers. Their website brings the history of canals and the fun of today together effectively. Kids can play interactive games, learn about wildlife and the waterways environment, discover how locks work, explore canal heritage and find loads to do and learn. The WOW tent also tours many of the waterways festivals and events, inviting kids to roll up their sleeves and play. Visit their website for a diary of events with kids in mind all around Britain's canals.

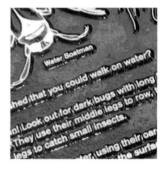

Details:
www.wow4water.net
Further info:
Visit their website to download free fact files and information packs and for lists of forthcoming events. Children aged 7-11 can also complete the five interactive safety activities of the Waterside Safety Challenge to learn the importance of the SAFE message - Stay Away From the Edge.

Pets too

You can let out a sigh of relief when it comes to days out and holidays on the waterways: forget kennels, pet sitters and the misery of leaving the hairiest member of the family behind. Canals are pet friendly. Take the whole family, to the water or to the towpath. Dogs make happy sailors, but quietly behind many a good dog, there lies a great cat too! Canine sailors will wag their way around the networks in brazen exuberance, while cats will sneak out after their boats moor up for the night. Look out for the giveaway cat flaps in many narrowboat doors, or peep behind the plant pots on decks of privately owned boats and you might catch a moggy snoozing till later. Spend long enough on the canals and you'll notice boats can be home for everything from parrots and budgies to hamsters (we've even seen chickens on one boat). Not all creatures take instantly to water travel, so know your pet. As well as boating breaks there are pet-friendly waterside B&Bs and cottages, canal events, walks, pubs and all the freedom of the great waterways outdoors.

Take your pet on a narrowboat holiday

Narrowboating holidays force you to slow down and unwind on the water, and the gentle escape from the stresses of modern life can be just as relaxing for four-legged holidaymakers too. Cruising along, the canine choice is whether to slip indoors for a snooze or sit on deck watching the world passing by. Then, when it's time to stretch the legs, just hop off onto the towpath. Cherish the company of your dog (or other pet) while you sip drinks and watch the sun go down together.

Details:
The majority of hireboat companies are happy for you to take your pet with you on holiday, subject to certain stipulations. Most make a small extra charge. See page 29 for details of hireboat companies around the country.

Tips before you go:
Check out dog-friendly pubs along your cruising route
Take your dog's own creature comforts from home (bed, food bowl, toys)
Plan your schedule so that you don't need to leave your dog alone on board
Check if your dog can swim and if not, get a dog life jacket (beware that decks can be slippery for paws so falling in is always a possibility, and even good swimmers can struggle to climb out of canal banks)
Make it a rule that your dog waits until the boat is fully moored before jumping off
Discourage your pet from drinking water from the canal
Pack a first aid kit, lead and make sure your dog's tag has waterproof contact details
Carry emergency vet details (it can be tricky finding vets from the canals)

A dog's own holiday

A barking idea, but an innovative alternative to kennels that your dog will love. If you're going somewhere and you can't take your dog, why not send your furry friend on a fun-packed narrowboat holiday of his own. A qualified beautician is aboard to tend to his paw-ship's needs and, between long walks, lazy evenings on deck and cosy nights tucked up in his cabin, it's probably as near doggie heaven as it gets.

Details:
Dog Holidays Afloat T:01278 699119 www.dogholidaysafloat.co.uk

Dog walks and walking breaks

Canal towpaths were originally for horses, but dogs can be forgiven for mistaking that they were made for them. Watch them run free and let off steam, winding down in idyllic surroundings, without the worry of sheep or cows. Canal walks, even in urban areas, are removed from the stress of death-mincing road traffic. Water dogs get the treat of a swim and agility experts can sprint over footbridges and scramble up and down the canal banks. The towpaths are a sociable place for dogs and no matter how bouncy, or retired, your dog is, there are endless walks with different doggie highlights. Why not go on a walking weekend or backpacking holiday with your dog, staying overnight in a dog-friendly canalside pub, B&B, cottage, hotel or campsite?

Details:
For a list of dog-friendly canalside accommodation, see page 141. Also see chapters on Hotels, B&Bs and Cottages. The majority of campsites are dog-friendly although it is worth checking before you go.

Tips

Doggie poo is never a glamorous topic. Leaving little Timmy's doings for the next unsuspecting pair of Clarks is a bitter act, despised by most dog lovers and loathers alike. Yet the trend of scooping the unmentionable into plastic bags is not the answer either, when it's flung into the canal or towpath hedgerow promising to hang around for a smelly 20 years. The solution is biodegradable bags taken home or disposed of in allocated dog waste bins, or there's nothing wrong with simply scooping the poo safely into the hedgerow with a stick from the towpath where it will naturally decompose within days if left open to the air.

DOG MOORING

And more...

Dog-friendly accommodation

Gliffaes Hotel: T:01874 730371
Crickhowell. Monmouthshire & Brecon Canal
www.gliffaes.co.uk Dogs welcome in special
kennels & around the grounds, not bedrooms

Lovat Arms: T:01456 459250/0845 4501100
Fort Augustus. Caledonian Canal. Allocated
room for pets www.lovatarms-hotel.com

Scotch Hall Cottage:
Trevor Basin, Llangollen Canal
T:01244 356695 www.sykescottages.co.uk

Darnley Cottage:
Pencelli. Monmouthshire & Brecon Canal
T:01873 810811 www.wiseinwales.co.uk 4-star

Hengwaithdy:
Overlooking canal near bridge 118
T:01873 810811 www.wiseinwales.co.uk 4-star

Highland Lodges:
Near Laggan Locks, Caledonian Canal. 3-star
T:01809 501225 www.highlandlodges.org.uk

Old Lock-House Apartments:
Two apartments by Fort Augustus locks
T:01784 482439 www.GoBarging.com

Coach House:
Ardrishaig. Crinan Canal
T:01546 603245 3-star

Foxtwood Cottages:
Canalside near Froghall Wharf. Caldon Canal
T:01538 266160 www.foxtwood.co.uk

More dog-friendly accommodation on
www.coolcanalsguides.com

Quirky adventures

Do something out of the ordinary. Eccentricity and extreme generosity are part of canal culture and the weird and wonderful seem drawn to the water. Abseiling the Falkirk Wheel for charity, murder mystery cruises in woolliest Scotland, jazz concerts inside a canal cave. On the waterways there are untold ways to seize the day, escape out of the box for fun, or do something you can feel proud of. This chapter invites you to do anything from the slightly wacky to the downright potty.

Dirty weekend

Not Bacardis by the beach, but definitely a holiday to remember. The Waterway Recovery Group organise canal camps throughout the year with weekend or week-long working holidays, where you'll be helping to restore derelict canals - doing anything from driving digger trucks to clearing muck from lock gates or cooking for around 20 camp mates. Roll up your sleeves and muck in, there's a job for everyone no matter what your skills. It's feisty fun. Do your bit for the canals and have the time of your life.

Details:
Waterway Recovery Group T:01494 783453 www.wrg.org.uk

Towpath Tidy

Don't got bogged down in the drudgery of spring-cleaning your house, get down on the towpaths with British Waterways and a bunch of volunteers to help with Towpath Tidy, the annual spring-clean. Crisp packets, cans, fishermen's litter, supermarket trolleys - the rubbish is a danger to wildlife and revolting to see. With over 150 tonnes worth of consumer carnage removed during each Towpath Tidy, every gloved helping hand is welcome.

Details:
Usually held in March. To find out how to volunteer, visit www.waterscape.com

Murder mystery cruise

For a different night out, go on a cruise that invites you to turn detective as you chomp on a meal spiced with villains and murder. All tongue in cheek of course!

Details:
Bath Narrowboats T:01225 447276 www.bath-narrowboats.co.uk
Bathwick, Bath. Kennet & Avon Canal OS ST757649

Details:
Bridge Inn T:0131 3331320 www.bridgeinn.com
Ratho. Union Canal OS NT139708

Run the ultra marathon

It's Britain's longest, toughest, and probably most overlooked, continuous race. If you fancy spending May Bank Holiday in the company of 80 or so runners, togged up with trainers, water bottles and hyper-thermal blankets, the rules are simple: all you have to do is run 145 miles within a time limit of 45 hours with no stops over 40 minutes. Marathons are a mere 26 miles but this is an ultra marathon so you have to be ultra-fit or ultra-bonkers to try it! If you do, and you successfully complete the distance within the time limit, you will have earned your title in the online hall of fame. If rising to the challenge sounds too sweaty for you, an alternative day out could involve a flask and fold-up chair, as you wave off the brave at the start in Birmingham, or count them back in at the finishing post in London. Just don't expect the numbers to tally - anything can happen between the start & the finish! One of the most electric drop-outs happened in 1998, when Sally Adams was struck by a bolt of lightning as she ran over Braunston Tunnel. Luckily she lived to tell the tale, and is now memorably known as 'Sparky Adams'. Thunder claps or not, the race is always eventful and a noteworthy day out, whether you're lycra fit or a couch potato.

Details:
Grand Union Canal Race T:01635 578536 www.gucr.co.uk
Start: Gas Street Basin, Birmingham OS SP062866 Finish: Little Venice, London OS TQ262818

Ceilidh on the water

If a narrowboat holiday on the tranquil waterways of England isn't enough for you, a barge on the Caledonian Canal in the Scottish Highlands might be. Throw in some wild Gaelic music, and a Ceilidh holiday aboard the 'Fingal of Caledonia' could become the ultimate experience, with not only musical antics, but sublime scenery too.

Details:
Fingal of Caledonia T:01397 772167 www.fingal-cruising.co.uk
Location:
Fort William. Caledonian Canal OS NN090766

And more...

Boat jumbles

Go bargain hunting! Boat jumbles are addictive and, even if you think you already have everything, some 'must have' is bound to leap out. Whether you sell or buy, or just go for a grand day out, boat jumbles are a great way to beat today's crazy throwaway culture.

Details:

Visit www.boatjumbleassociation.co.uk for a calendar of Boat Jumbles across the country

Get active for charity

Abseiling the Falkirk Wheel for charity might not be your cup of tea, but there are plenty of other ways to do your bit and get the feel-good factor. Whether you want to raise money for charity, help restore a canal or protect waterways wildlife, you can make a difference. Join in and help save both our waterways and the earth.

Further info:

Waterscape covers many of the organised events with information on how to get involved www.waterscape.com

Wild and free

A sanctuary with miles of hedgerows, trees, flowers & grasses, insects, fish, birds and water-loving animals. It's almost ironic that a man-made transport route has become a natural haven for wildlife in the countryside and an oasis of nature in urban landscapes, with over 1,000 wildlife conservation sites and 65 Sites of Special Scientific Interest. It is probably impossible to visit the waterways and ignore the wildlife - whether you just catch a robin from the corner of your eye, share your crusts with a duck family, or snatch a glimpse of an otter. Herons, swans, ducks, geese, kingfishers and moorhens mingle into a cacophony of hierarchies with inevitable squabbles over feathered territories. Get outdoors with nature.

Go wild on your nearest canal

The great thing about canals is that you don't have to travel to the other end of the country to find a wealth of wildlife. Nip to your nearest waterway, and discover its own secret life of insects, herons, geese, frogs, moorhens, the humble duck and much more. Tiptoe onto the towpaths at dawn and watch water life secretly waking, or go at dusk and you could bump into a bat or two under bridges and among the trees. Any canal is an untamed, man-made beauty spot. Go for the day, walk among wildflowers and butterflies on the towpaths, then picnic or stop off at the pub.

Wild day on the Pocklington Canal in Yorkshire

The Pocklington Canal is a designated Site of Special Scientific Interest and one of the most important canals in the UK for wildlife because it is home to a diversity of plants, animals and birds. Its lily-clad waters bluster with dragonflies and damselflies and, where branches overhang, you may strike the blue glint of a kingfisher perching for fish. Otters hide elusively and shy birds from wagtails to sedge warblers swoop the landscape.

Day on the Lancaster Canal in Lancashire

The Lancaster Canal brags views across Morecambe Bay to the high fells of the Lake District. The Glasson Branch is the only link with the sea, cutting through idyllic countryside vital for breeding and migrating birds such as mute swans, ducks, coot, great-crested grebe and many types of gull. In winters, whooper and Bewick's swans sometimes linger and curlews love the sandbanks of the estuary. Visit any time of year for a genuine waterways experience dosed with wetland birds and wildflowers.

Details:
To find your nearest canal and more information on the Pocklington Canal, the Lancaster Canal and wildlife, visit www.waterscape.com

Swans

The angels of the waterways, revered for their elegance and majestic beauty; yet look beyond their blanched aura and you'll see individual characters and giant souls. In flight swans can reach incredible speeds of 55mph and being witness to the take-off is a heart-stopping privilege: the frenzied run on the water, building into the full glory of white flight, echoed by a deep, slow, rhythmic 'whoosh-whoosh' of feathered aerodynamics. It is the simplest wonder of the waterways world.

Herons

You'll spy these shy, lanky birds fishing on the canal banks and, like the pot at the end of the rainbow, you never quite reach them before they fly off.

Ducks

Water is just water without a crowd of ducks.

Geese

Gaggles of geese, honking and flapping in the water, are a sight to see, but be there at dawn or dusk to witness their simultaneous flight. A moment of genuine goose bumps.

Water voles

One of Britain's endangered species, the water vole clings to survival finding sanctuary in secluded banks along canals. Listen for a distinctive 'plop' breaking the silence from the water, it may be the vole swimming for his supper. Voles get confused with the less glamorous rat so watch out for small ears, silky brown fur, short furry tail and cute rounded nose.

Coots and moorhens

Coots and moorhens look similar and are often mistakenly identified. Coots are black with a white beak and bold white patch on the front of their heads while moorhens are black with a mostly red beak.

And more...

The Wildlife Trusts

Wildlife Trusts are looking for help with the threatened water vole, asking visitors to the waterways to report any sightings online.
T:01636 677711 www.wildlifetrusts.org

Swan Sanctuary

Canals would be a lesser place without swans, yet water pollution, vandalism, uncontrolled dogs, litter, fishing tackle and lead poisoning are among some of the threats they face every day. Visitors to the canal can be at the frontline of reporting injured swans and get rescue services to their aid as quickly as possible. Be sure to carry the emergency number with you.

Details:
National Swan Sanctuary T:01784 431667
RSPCA T:08705 555999

Worcester & Slimbridge

Worcester has a thriving community of swans, mostly due to the dedicated work of the local Swan Sanctuary. Swans gather in their hundreds near where the Worcester & Birmingham Canal meets the river Severn. Further down the river Severn, parallel with the Gloucester & Sharpness Canal, swans frequent Slimbridge. Visit between November and February to enjoy floodlit swan feeds.

Details:
Slimbridge Wildfowl & Wetlands Trust
T:01453 891900 www.wwt.org.uk

National Waterway Wildlife Survey

Organised by British Waterways and Waterscape, their annual survey tracks sightings of a variety of species, including dragonflies, kingfishers and badgers.
All information supplied by the public is inputted into a wildlife database to help with conservation work. www.waterscape.com

Waterside camping

Sleep under the stars and let the ducks wake you. That's canalside camping. The philosophy is simple: less is more. Arrive by water road, pitch your tent and allow yourself to sit and stare. After an all-day adventure by canoe, on foot or by bike, pull the rucksack from your back and unravel your home for the night. This sort of camping spoils you with freedom from possessions and the luxury of a bivvy supper under the stars, ready for an early dawn start tomorrow. Of course you can always cheat and bring your tent, comfiest pillows, fold-up sink and crate of wine by car! Whether you plan to pitch your tent and explore from base camp, or tour from A to B, canalside campsites can be the most flexible and casual way to holiday independently with all the freedom of the outdoors.

Camp on the farm

A steep hill along the Kennet and Avon Canal transforms into an amazing 16-lock experience at Caen Hill. By boat, bike, boot or wheelchair it's one of Wiltshire's many 'magical' highlights and officially one of the7 wonders of the waterways. The towpath along this stretch is particularly well maintained for easy, year-round cycling and walking. Lower Foxhangers Farm sits canalside at the bottom of the flight and offers everything from a pitch for your tent to self-catering mobile homes, narrowboat hire and even B&B in the farmhouse.

Details:
Lower Foxhangers Farm T:01380 828254 www.foxhangers.com
Location:
By lock 23, Devizes. Kennet & Avon Canal OS ST966613
What's in the area?
Caen Hill Locks (see page 243) and Devizes

Severn way

Grab the drama of an under-sung canal. Tall ships, swans, Saul Junction and possibly the Severn Bore in the distance are some of the sights to see from the Gloucester & Sharpness. Tudor Caravan Park sits next to the canal, just a short walk from the world-famous Slimbridge Wildfowl and Wetlands Trust. Wildlife and conservation lie close to the Park's heart and they have won a Gold David Bellamy Conservation Award for the last 9 years. They're open all year, so wrap up warm and enjoy.

Details:
Tudor Caravan Park T:01453 890483 www.tudorcaravanpark.co.uk
Location:
By Patch Bridge, Slimbridge. Gloucester & Sharpness Canal OS ST966613
What's in the area?
Slimbridge, the Severn Way and a CAMRA award-winning pub next door
Further info:
AA 3 Pennant & Gold David Bellamy Conservation Award

Camp in the mountains

The peace and quiet of the Monmouthshire & Brecon Canal is perfect for stopovers. Whether you're touring with a camper van, caravan or backpacking by foot or bike, Pencelli is 5-star camping not to miss - with awards coming out of its ears, including the prestigious 'Loo of the year' award 2008. The aesthetics of your individual experience are respected as tents and caravans are tactfully separated by hedging. If you want to tuck yourself in an earthy corner and snuggle up in a sleeping bag to watch the moon rise, you can. Arriving late from the towpaths, with a tent on your back, no one will care if you cheat and warm up with a hot chocolate from the coined machine in the campsite's spanking clean utility rooms. This site has a great atmosphere and offers a canalside camping experience at any time of year in the beautiful Brecon Beacons. Hard to beat.

Details:
Pencelli Castle Campsite T:01874 665451 www.pencelli-castle.com
Location:
By bridge 153, Pencelli. Monmouthshire & Brecon Canal OS SO092249
What's in the area?
Brecon Beacons National Park all around, Brecon 5 miles along the towpath (see page 51)
Further info:
5-star, Gold David Bellamy Conservation Award, Loo of the Year 2008

Camp at the pub

The setting is an ancient leafy landscape, riddled with crop circle magic, where you'd expect to see the local bobby cheerily cycling the windy lanes. At the Barge Inn you get a great historic canal pub, one of Britain's prettiest canals and a campsite all rolled into one. Pitch up with views beyond the canal to the White Horse of Alton Barnes. Don't bother bringing your travel iron - facilities are basic, but the appeal is enormous.

Details:
The Barge Inn T:01672 851705 www. the-barge-inn.com. Dogs welcome
Location:
Honeystreet, Pewsey. Kennet & Avon Canal OS SU103615

And more...

Canal Side Caravan Site: T:01948 663284
By bridge 28, Grindley Brook. Llangollen Canal
www.canalsidecaravansite.20m.com

Gilestone Caravan Park: T:01874 676236
Near Talybont-on-Usk. Mon & Brec Canal
www.gilestonecaravanpark.co.uk 4-star

Fort Augustus Caravan Park: T:01320 366618
Short walk from canal. Caledonian Canal
www.campinglochness.co.uk 4-star No tents

Lochgilphead Caravan Park: T:01546 602003
Near Oakfield Swing Bridge. Crinan Canal
www.lochgilpheadcaravanpark.co.uk

Glencote Caravan Park: T: 01538 360745
Near Basford Bridge. Caldon Canal. 5-star
www.glencote.co.uk Gold Conservation Award

Wigrams Campsite: T:01926 810310/303
Napton. Junction Oxford/Grand Union Canals
www.wigramscanalside.co.uk

Little Stubbins Caravan Park: T:01995 640376
Near bridge 51, Lancaster Canal. No tents
www.littlestubbins.co.uk B&B (see page 181)

Canal Visitor Centre: T:01252370073
Mytchett. Basingstoke Canal. Need to prebook
www.basingstoke-canal.org.uk

Minnows Touring Park: T:01884 821770
Sampford Peverell. Grand Western Canal
www.ukparks.co.uk/minnows

Golden Valley: T:01773 513881
Cromford Canal. DB Gold Conservation Award
www.goldenvalleycaravanpark.co.uk 4-star

More camping on www.coolcanalsguides.com

Hot hotels

Hotels make a relaxing stopover along the waterways and are the perfect base for exploring. The world of canals is all about water, and narrowboats of course, yet sleeping somewhere special on the canals can be surprisingly creative. Why not book into a great waterside hotel, then either stay in one place or hotel hop along the water's edge. Sleep at the wharf in city style or stay in the middle of nowhere. Discover quirky, small and friendly hotels, the best budget or go the whole hog and luxuriate in 5-star style. Or try a hotel boat. It's the perfect hotel that moves along the waterways with you. Pamper yourself.

Hotel narrowboats and barges

It's the great gentle break. During the day choose whether to pick up a glass of wine or a windlass, and after dusk let someone else make dinner and do the washing up. Later, when you've chatted enough, fall asleep to the relaxing sounds of silence. Hotel boats usually operate with an intimate family-run ethos and there's always a warm welcome whether you arrive solo or not. The random chance of who you share your holiday with is part of the buzz, but if the risk sounds ghastly to you, some boats do group bookings. Most hotel boats have a set cruising itinerary covering different rings throughout the year. There are lots of different types of boat to choose from, wide beam or narrow. Often traditional hotel narrowboats work as a pair: one boat with an engine pulls a non-motorized butty. Of course, whatever style of boat and wherever the route, you can choose to muck in with the crew, help out at locks or learn fancy rope work. You can usually plan your day around your own interests. Stay aboard, enjoy a leisurely stroll along the towpath or, if you're feeling more energetic, use the boat as a handy Sherpa to carry your baggage and greet you with supper after a long day's hike. A hotel boat holiday suits the sociable and the convivial possibilities are endless. Expect to be pampered with the slow luxuries of life, while basking in the pleasure of water travel.

Away4awhile: Single narrowboat. Sleeps 6 T:0845 6445144 www.away4awhile.co.uk 3-star
Boatel Experience: Widebeam barge. Sleeps 4 T:07804 454074
Bywater Hotelboat Cruises: Traditional pair. Sleeps 8 T:07775 850098 www.bywaterhotelboats.co.uk
Canal Voyagers: Traditional boat pair. Sleeps 9 T:07921 214414 www.canalvoyagers.com 4-star
Duke & Duchess: Traditional boat pair. Sleeps 8 T:07711 836441 www.hotelboat-holidays.co.uk 4-star
English Holiday Cruises: Edward Elgar Slps 22 T:0845 6017895 www.englishholidaycruises.co.uk
Fingal of Caledonia: Converted barge. Sleeps 12 T:01397 772167 www.fingal-cruising.co.uk
Gallinago Barge Holidays: Widebeam barge. Sleeps 4 T:07831 110811 www.barge-cruises.com
Go Barging: Luxury all-inclusive hotel-barges in the UK & Europe T:01784 482439 www.gobarging.com
LadyLine Hotel Boats: Two boats. Sleep 8 T:07986 133122 www.ladylinehotelboats.co.uk 4-star
Periwinkle: Single narrowboat. Sleeps 3 T:07747 017263 www.hotelboatperiwinkle.com 4-star
Reed Boats: Traditional hotelboat pair. Sleeps 8 T:07977 229103 www.reedboats.co.uk 4-star
Shadow Cruisers: Traditional hotelboat pair. Sleeps 4 T:07966 753356 www.shadowcruisers.f9.co.uk
Tranquil Rose: Widebeam barge. Sleeps 9 T:07966 248079 www.tranquilrose.co.uk 4-star
Willow: Single narrowboat. Sleeps 2. Private charter only T:07702 242100 www.hotelnarrowboat.com
Wood Owl: Single narrowboat. Sleeps 4 T:07981 798272 www.woodowl.co.uk

Posh pillows

It doesn't get much grander than this. England's second city, capital of the canal world, and one of the plushest hotels along Britain's canals. Birmingham's Hyatt Hotel is definitely a room with a view, dramatically overlooking Water's Edge and Gas Street Basin (see pages 192-199).

Details:
Hyatt Regency Birmingham T:0121 6431234 www.birmingham.regency.hyatt.com 4-star
Location:
Bridge Street, Birmingham. Birmingham Canal Navigations OS SP062866

Camden nights

Since London's hippy 70s it has been a cool Sunday tradition to chill out, gongoozling, at Camden Lock, just letting life happen. There are crafts and colourful bargains in the famous markets, waterside bars and restaurants, street music and enough atmosphere to make you linger for the night life. The canalside 4-star Holiday Inn has rooms with views over Camden Lock.

Details:
Holiday Inn T:0207 4854343 www.holidayinncamden.co.uk 4-star
Location:
Camden Lock, London. Regent's Canal OS TQ285839

Sleep in an art gallery

You've reached the Outdoor Capital of Britain, at the foot of Ben Nevis, near the Caledonian Canal. If breathing the West Highland scenery makes going indoors seem a waste, even for sleep, stay in the hotel that brings the landscape indoors. The Lime Tree is not just a stylish hotel, it's an impressive art gallery too. Rooms are decorated with art of the stunning outdoors and a dedicated gallery space hosts artwork you can view or buy.

Details:
The Lime Tree T:01397 701806 www.limetreefortwilliam.co.uk 3-star
Location:
Fort William. Loch Linnhe near the Caledonian Canal OS NN095732

And more...

Moat House Hotel: T:01785 712217
Acton Trussell. Staffs & Worcs Canal
www.moathouse.co.uk 4-star Grade 11-listed

Dunsley Hall Hotel: T:01384 877077
Kinver. Staffs & Worcs Canal. Grade 11-listed
www.dunsleyhallhotel.co.uk Cat Stanley's blog

Royal Station Hotel: T:01524 732033
Carnforth. Lancaster Canal. Opposite railway
station setting of film 'Brief Encounter'. 2-star

Five Rise Locks Hotel: T:01274 565296
Bingley. Leeds & Liverpool Canal
www.five-rise-locks.co.uk Dog-friendly

Rendezvous Hotel: T:01756 700100
By bridge 181, Leeds & Liverpool Canal
www.rendezvous-skipton.com 3-star

Crinan Hotel: T:01546 830261 (see page 117)
Crinan by Lochgilphead. Crinan Canal
www.crinanhotel.com Dog-friendly

Braunston Manor: T:01788 890267
Near bridge 91, Grand Union Canal
www.braunstonmanor.co.uk 4-star & Awards

Moorings Hotel: T:01397 772797
Neptune's Staircase, Caledonian Canal. 3-star
www.moorings-fortwilliam.co.uk Dog-friendly

Falcon Hotel: T:01288 352005
Bude. Bude Canal. Alfred Lord Tennyson broke
a leg when staying here! www.falconhotel.com

Bryn Howel Hotel: T:01978 860331
By bridge 38, Llangollen Canal Dog-friendly
www.brynhowel.com 3-star. Disabled access

More hotels on www.coolcanalsguides.com

Waterside and floating B&Bs

The great British B&B is all the rage again and now it's not about over-fried eggs and chintz. Canals go the extra mile when it comes to offering a great B&B - it's not just waterside accommodation, it's floating B&Bs too. Waterways hospitality comes packed with character and that's especially true if you stay in a narrowboat B&B. Whether you stay on land or water, B&Bs are the convenient way to travel the waterways on a budget. A comfy bed for the night, followed by a full English and you're back on your way. Some B&Bs will even create a packed lunch for your day too. There's no need to lug a tent around in a heavy rucksack and you don't have to think about the washing up! So whether you're a six-star plumped-up pillow person, or an earthy billycan type, there's a B&B for you.

Sleep by the marina

Braunston is the water crossroads between north and south, where the Grand Union and Oxford Canals meet. The picturesque marina is an infamous hub of boat activity, with a chandlery, shop, boat yard, boat hire and rows of colourful moored boats. At the marina, the Old Workshop is a quiet 4-star B&B with green credentials and, as they are participants in the Walkers Welcome and Cyclists Welcome scheme, you're guaranteed a warm welcome if you arrive by boot or bike.

Details:
The Old Workshop, Braunston T:01788 891421 www.the-old-workshop.com
Location:
Braunston Marina, Grand Union Canal OS SP544658
Further info:
4-star Eco-friendly Walkers/Cyclists Welcome
What's in the area?
You're right in the marina so boats are everywhere and you're a short walk from the village

Sleep on the canal bank

While everyone else in the Brecon Beacons is climbing mountains, hiking through the National Park, mountain biking, canoeing, bird watching, moseying around craft shops, horse riding or playing golf, you can escape to the simple peace and quiet of the canal. When night comes, if sleeping alfresco on the canal bank sounds a ridiculous idea, stay at the Canal Bank, a smart 5-star canalside B&B in Brecon.

Details:
Canal Bank, Brecon T:01874 623464 www.accommodation-breconbeacons.co.uk
Location:
Near Watton Bridge, Monmouthshire & Brecon Canal OS SO047281
Further info:
5-star Gold Award. See page 51 for a walk on the Mon & Brec Canal
What's in the area?
Stunning scenery along the canal in one direction, a short walk into Brecon town centre in the other

Birmingham's floating B&B

For an alternative winter B&B, stay in the heart of Birmingham's canals on Away2stay, the city's funky floating B&B where you can drift off to sleep on the water after enjoying the parallel glitz of urban nightlife.

Details:
Away2stay T:0845 6445144 www.away2stay.co.uk
Location:
The Mailbox, Birmingham. Worcester & Birmingham Canal OS SP064863
Further info:
Hotel boat moored at The Mailbox for winter (October to March). 3-star
What's in the area?
The Mailbox is at the heart of Birmingham's canals (see pages 193-199 for more info)

Night with Nessie

Wake up where the Caledonian Canal swells into Loch Ness and the attraction of Scotland's coast-to-coast waterway is at its most potent. The Pottery House is a 4-star B&B with Green Tourism awards, offering full Scottish breakfasts, homemade jams and not a battery egg in sight. You may even be lucky and spy an elusive red squirrel scurrying in the garden.

Details:
Pottery House, Dores T:01463 751267 www.potteryhouse.co.uk
Location:
Dores, Caledonian Canal OS NH598347
Further info:
4-star. Green Tourism Gold Award. Winner of Highlands Tourism Award 2008
What's in the area?
You're on the shore of Loch Ness, stunning scenery and walks galore all around you

Elizabeth Rose floating B&B

Space inside a narrowboat can be intimate, but the Elizabeth Rose offers a smart private double cabin, personal bathroom and private deck at the front of the boat, just a friendly call away from the crew at the rear. All mod cons, full English and a 2-hour cruise for overnight stays.

Details:
Elizabeth Rose T:07974 861166 www.the-elizabethrose.co.uk Mainly along the Trent & Mersey Canal

And more...

Rectory Cottage: T:01495 785712
Mamhilad. Mon & Brec Canal 4-star
www.walesbnb.com Walkers/Cyclists Welcome

White House: T:01691 658524
Maesbury Marsh. Montgomery Canal
www.maesburymarsh.co.uk 4-star Vegetarian

Rhiw Goch: T:01397 772373
Banavie. Caledonian Canal
www.rhiwgoch.co.uk By Neptune's Staircase

Waterways Cottage: T:01604 863865
Stoke Bruerne. Grand Union Canal
www.waterwayscottage.co.uk

Wharf Cottage: T:01527 559339
Stoke Prior. Worcester & Birmingham Canal
www.wharfcottagebromsgrove.co.uk Log cabin

Little Stubbins: T:01995 640376 see page 165
Near bridge 51. Lancaster Canal 4-star
Walkers/Cyclists Welcome. Dog-friendly

Laurel End House: T:01422 846980
Hebden Bridge. Rochdale Canal. Dog-friendly
www.laurelend.com Vegetarian options

Tolley Cottage: T:01225 463365
Bath. Kennet & Avon Canal. Organic, locally
sourced breakfasts www.tolleycottage.co.uk

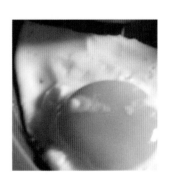

Breakwater House: T:01288 353137
Near the sea lock, Bude. Bude Canal
www.breakwaterhouse.co.uk 5-star

Mountain Oak Farm: T:01884 820053
Sampford Peverell. Grand Western Canal
www.mountainoakfarm.co.uk Fresh local food

More B&Bs on www.coolcanalsguides.com

Cottages, mills and cosy retreats

To go for the day is great, but to stay is even better. After the gentle hubbub of the day, the waterways become yours. You're free to watch the moon rise over the water, and eat supper in a special place, before falling asleep soothed in the ambience of a waterways night. For an authentic experience, steep yourself in the real world of the waterways and stay in a historic lock-keeper's cottage or relax in the ambience of an old converted waterside mill. Cosy retreats don't have to be hundreds of years old though; wharfside self-catering apartments are available with fully-fitted contemporary panache. So sleep snugly on the waterside. Soak up the stillness after dusk and wake to the dawn chorus of ducks and geese and the clinking of mooring rings as narrowboaters untie their ropes. Then saunter into the kitchen for your eggs sunny side up.

Stratford bed in a barrel

Lengthsmen in the early 1800s usually looked after one lock and the stretch of water as far as the next. Engineers building the Stratford-on-Avon Canal knew more about building bridges than houses, so when they had to build lock cottages for the lengthsmen, they adapted their skills, resulting in cottages with curious barrel-shaped roofs. Creaking with history, cosy open fires in winter and a sociable lock-side vantage point, the Lengthsman's Cottage at Lowsonford has all the promise of a memorable experience.

Details:
Lengthsman's Cottage. Landmark Trust T:01628 825925 www.landmarktrust.org.uk
Location:
By lock 31, Lowsonford. Stratford-on-Avon Canal OS SP189677
What's in the area?
Fleur de Lys pub just across the canal and a 4-mile towpath walk to Wootton Wawen

Tardebigge flight

Rolling Worcestershire fields with Elgar's Malvern Hills as a backdrop make this stretch of the Worcester & Birmingham Canal a surprisingly beautiful place to stay. This canal boasts the longest lock flight in Britain, with 30 locks to climb from Stoke Pound to Tardebigge Top Lock. Mid-flight overnight mooring is not allowed, so boaters must grab their windlasses, roll up their sleeves and earnestly take to the tiller. After the slog, they can moor up either end to recover for a night. Luckily there is a lazier way to sleep on the Tardebigge. Just snuggle up in comfort between locks 31 and 32, for a relaxing night (or longer) at Lock Cottage. Don't forget to wave at boaters as they pass by!

Details:
Lock Cottage. Landmark Trust T:01628 825925 www.landmarktrust.org.uk
Location:
By lock 31, Tardebigge. Worcester & Birmingham Canal OS SO966679
What's in the area?
Stunning countryside, towpath walks and a pub a short walk away

Room at the inn

Ronnie the Labrador will welcome you to Longlands Hotel, a family run inn & restaurant, sitting next to the disused Tewitfield Locks at the northern end of the Lancaster Canal. Longlands Hotel describes itself as "comfortably contemporary with a country twist" and offers good beer and food to the leisurely traveller. They have been awarded the Taste Lancashire mark of quality for their food and because they are independent from chain pubs and hotels it's safe to expect the genuine thing. You can choose to sleep in one of the hotel rooms or one of their self-catering stone cottages with breakfast in the hotel included.

Details:
Longlands Hotel T:01524 781256 www.longlandshotel.co.uk
Location:
By Tewitfield Locks, Tewitfield. Lancaster Canal OS SD519736
Further info:
Dog-friendly
What's in the area?
4 towpath miles south to Morecambe Bay or 15 miles north to Kendal and the Lake District

Luxury Highland apartments

If you fancy touring the Caledonian Canal from a comfortable base, the luxury 5-star canalside apartments overlooking Neptune's Staircase might woo you. All the apartments are contemporary and slick but, if you're feeling ultra spoilt or downright naughty, the Penthouse Suite not only overlooks the canal but flings spectacular views of Ben Nevis at you too.

Details:
Canalside Apartments T:07786 966245 www.highlandholidayapartments.co.uk
Location:
By Neptune's Staircase, Banavie. Caledonian Canal OS NN114771
Further info:
5-star. Dog-friendly
What's in the area?
Stunning scenery, towpath walks, Fort William and outdoor activities galore

And more...

Croft Mill Apartments: T:01422 846836 4-star
Hebden Bridge. Rochdale Canal. Walkers/
Cyclists/Families Welcome. www.croftmill.com

Skipton Canal Cottage: T:01253 347740
Skipton. Leeds & Liverpool Canal
www.skiptoncanalcottage.co.uk

The Canal Barn: T:01380 728883
2 cottages by Caen Hill. Kennet & Avon Canal
www.canalbarn.co.uk Disabled access

Folly Cottages: T:01788 891410
Behind Folly Inn, Napton. Oxford Canal
www.follycottages.com Dog-friendly

No 3 Aqueduct Cottages: T:07971 247419
Chirk Bank. Llangollen Canal. Former canal
worker's cottage www.chirkcottage.co.uk

Whipcott Water Cottages: T:01823 672339
Grand Western Canal. Disabled access. 4-star
www.oldlimekilncottages.co.uk Dog-friendly

Waterside Bungalow: T:01204 882580
Bolton-le-Sands. Lancaster Canal. 4-star
www.watersidebungalow.co.uk Dog-friendly

The Barn: T:01384 390520
Near Stourton. Stourbridge Canal
www.blackcountrystays.com 4-star

Seangan Croft: T:0141 5890014
Muirshearlich. Caledonian Canal. Dog-friendly
www.seangan.co.uk 3-star cottages & lodges

Counting House: T:01874 676446
Talybont-on-Usk. Mon & Brec Canal. 2-star
www.breconcottages.com Historic canal house

More cottages on www.coolcanalsguides.com

Birmingham

London usually towers its shadow over England's second city, Birmingham, but in the canal world Birmingham is the bona fide capital of Britain. Right in the heart of England, 200 spaghetti miles of city canal networks outrival a certain suave city in Italy. Visitors come to Brum to experience the shopping metropolis, to get a flavour of the infamous Balti houses, to scrutinize controversial new architecture, to stand by Anthony Gormley's Iron Man or simply to soak up the cosmopolitan Brummie culture. Meanwhile, as urban tourists try to cram in as much as they can, the canals carry on winding down in their secret parallel world peacefully ignoring the drums of the city. Those in the know can peep over the bridge, look down from the busy street and venture into the slow city.

Brindley Place

Brindley Place is a one-stop therapeutic dose of water calm and a mecca for waterways tourism. Commuter cyclists, walkers, shoppers, tourists and, at certain times of day, suited city workers, melt into urban gongoozlers enjoying the linear park like mini New Yorkers. Bars, cafés, restaurants and shops all vie for your attention, while the Mediterranean-style outdoor culture invites you to enjoy the canal and its passing boats. Art and culture abound. The Ikon Gallery, International Convention Centre, Symphony Hall, National Indoor Arena and National Sealife Centre are all overlooking or within walking distance of the canal.

Details:
Brindley Place T:0121 6436866 www.brindleyplace.com OS SP061866

Gas Street Basin

Brindley Place flows into an area known as Gas Street Basin, once the epicentre of the Industrial Revolution where narrowboats loaded and unloaded cargoes of coal, glass and chocolate crumb. The zone was so important in its former heyday that it became the first area in Birmingham to be lit by gaslights (a clue to its name). The surprise of this oasis, a million metaphysical miles from the glitzy city, is that it lures your mind to a bygone Birmingham and dares you to sink into a chair at one of the waterside cafes to let time pass by, just for a waterways while!

Details:
Gas Street Basin. More information on www.waterscape.com OS SP062866

Guided walks

Take a walk back in time with one of British Waterways' guides, who will help you uncover clues to the history of Birmingham's canals. Walks run throughout the summer.

Details:
British Waterways Visitor Information Centre, Cambrian Wharf T:0121 6326845

The Mailbox

Once the Royal Mail sorting office, the Mailbox is the place to go for designer shopping, café bars, waterside restaurants and hotels. Birmingham is notoriously multicultural and its waterside is home to world cuisine. With tastes of Paris, Thailand, India, sushi and tapas, you're spoilt for choice and there's no Mcdonald's. Sip cocktails in the Mailbox and hobnob in style.

Details:
The Mailbox T:0121 6321000 www.mailboxlife.com OS SP064863
Further info:
After 32 years at Pebble Mill, the Mailbox became home to BBC Birmingham in 2004. They now offer guided tours behind the scenes, bookable on T:0370 9011227

Canalside Adventure Trail

For children, Ollie the Otter's Canalside Adventure Trail starts at Brindley Place, walks through Gas Street Basin and finishes by the National Sealife Centre. Otters keep themselves to themselves so if you don't see Ollie on the walk, you'll definitely see some of his friends in the Sealife Centre.

Details:
Leaflets available from British Waterways Visitor Information Centre, Cambrian Wharf T:0121 6326845

Waterbus and boat trips

Tour Birmingham by boat for a different view of the city. Catching the bus is more glamorous than normal when you hop on the waterbus bobbing along Birmingham's city centre canals. Short boat trips also depart from the quayside by the International Convention Centre every day from Easter to October, and weekends in winter. Themed trips such as Valentine's and Santa cruises operate at special times throughout the year too.

Details:
Sherborne Wharf Heritage Narrowboats T:0121 4556163 www.sherbornewharf.co.uk The company operate boat trips, boat hire, the waterbus and even the Floating Coffee Company (see page 87)

Further info:
Tourist Information Centre: Birmingham T:0844 8883883 www.marketingbirmingham.com
More info on Birmingham's canals and other canals - www.waterscape.com

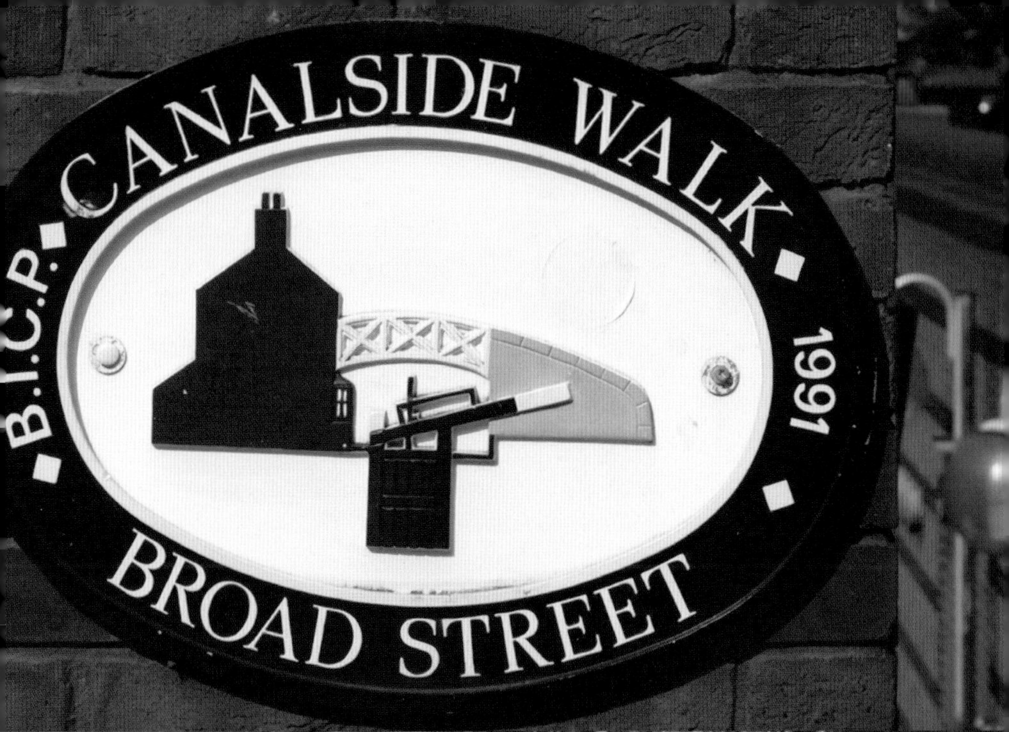
CANALSIDE WALK
B.I.C.P.
1991
BROAD STREET

National Indoor Arena
handmade burger Co
BIRMINGHAM
Oasis Too

And more...

Sleep

Hyatt Hotel: (see page 170)
Overlooking Gas Street Basin

Premier Inn:
Bridge Street. Canalside near Worcester Bar
T:08701 977031 www.premierinn.com

Ramada Hotel: T:0121 6439344
The Mailbox. Overlooking the canal
www.ramadabirminghamcity.co.uk

Away2stay: (see page 178)
Hotel boat at The Mailbox

Eat & drink

Away2dine:
Cruising restaurant (see page 73)

Floating Coffee Company: (see page 87)
Moored at Brindley Place

Canalside Café: (see page 86)
Canalside at Worcester Bar

James Brindley:
Canalside at Gas Street Basin
T:0121 6445971

Malt House:
Canalside by Old Turn, Brindley Place
T:0121 6334171

Tap & Spile: T:0121 6325602
Canalside by Gas Street Basin
www.tapandspilebirmingham.co.uk

The Mailbox: (see page 196)
Numerous restaurants & bars

Llangollen

On the north Wales borderlands you'll find the canal town of Llangollen. At first glance the town appears typically Celtic and modest, but look even closer and you'll spot it wailing with stunning scenery and one of the world's extraordinary engineering marvels. The Llangollen Canal is 46 miles long with plenty for the visitor to see and do along the whole waterway. The highlight of this canal is the Pontcysyllte Aqueduct, one of the most spectacular engineering feats of Britain's entire canal network. Secretly Llangollen knows its worth today and in town tourists can catch fringes of commercialism, but that's easily forgotten when you head off the beaten track following the canal to explore the surrounding countryside.

Festival capital

Llangollen isn't shy about its reputation as the festival capital of Wales. Most famously it belts multi-coloured music across the landscape during its International Music Eisteddfod. The festival field is just alongside the canal and when the world arrives in Llangollen to sing, it's thrilling. Throughout the year the town bursts with less well-known festivals too. The Fringe Festival carries on from the Eisteddfod to the end of July, then there's the jazz festival, the balloon festival, the food festival, the Christmas festival: almost anything is a good reason to party in this corner of Wales. Choose carefully when you go if you want the place to yourself.

Further info:
International Music Eisteddfod July www.eisteddfod-ryngwladol.co.uk
Fringe Festival Last two weeks in July www.llangollenfringe.co.uk

Pontcysyllte Aqueduct

Nothing prepares you for the drama of the Pontcysyllte Aqueduct, one of the 7 Wonders of Britain's inland waterways. 18 pillars, still held together by ox blood and Welsh flannel after 200 years, stretch to the heavens keeping the Llangollen Canal miraculously suspended 127 feet above the river Dee. Only two types of people ever travel across the aqueduct – the vertiginous and the non-vertiginous. There is no escaping the adrenalin of sheer drops either side with no more than a slither of towpath clinging to the narrow trough of water and the intangible haze of wind between you and the river valley below.

Details:
Pontcysyllte Aqueduct. Built by Thomas Telford and William Jessop, it was completed in 1805.
Location:
Trevor Basin. Llangollen Canal OS SJ270420
Further info:
The Pontcysyllte Aqueduct and part of the Llangollen Canal have been nominated for World Heritage status with the decision to be announced in 2009. See 7 Wonders on page 243.

Boats

Llangollen Wharf is the starting point for boat trips along the canal to Pontcysllte Aqueduct. One of the last few horse-drawn boats in the UK travels in the other direction, towards the end of the canal at Horseshoe Falls. The horses are friendly and will let the kids get close (the crew say their horses are fearless and only scared by umbrellas!). There's also a small tea room selling canalia and homemade cake.

Details:
Horse-drawn Boats, Llangollen Wharf T:01978 860702 www.horsedrawnboats.co.uk
Enjoy a 45-minute horse-drawn boat trip. Also boat trips to and across the Pontcysyllte Aqueduct in the motorised boat Thomas Telford, with informative commentary. Various trip options. (See pages 35 & 38)

Plas Nywedd

Two genteel ladies, known as the Ladies of Llangollen, escaped convention in the 18th century when they ran away together and downsized from the riches of society to live their dreams together for 50 years. You can tour the house and grounds. Marginally voyeuristic, but fascinating historically.

Details:
Plas Newydd T:01978 861314 www.denbighshire.gov.uk

Llangollen heritage railway

The Llangollen railway is a mainly steam-hauled heritage railway line which follows the river Dee for 7½ miles to Carrog. They operate special themed trips such as 'A day out with Thomas' during school holidays, and Steam Railway Experience days for train enthusiasts.

Details:
Llangollen Railway T:01978 860979 www.llangollen-railway.co.uk Café and shop in the station, just below the canal. Operated most weekends throughout the year and weekdays from June to September

Further info:
For a cycle ride from Llangollen to Pontcysyllte Aqueduct, see page 64
Boat hire: Anglo Welsh Waterway Holidays, Trevor Basin by Pontcysyllte T:0117 3041122
Tourist Information Centre: Llangollen T:01978 860828 www.visitwales.com
More info on Llangollen Canal and other canals - www.waterscape.com

And more...

Sleep

Ty Camlas B&B:
Canalside near Llangollen Wharf. 3-star
T:01978 861969 www.tycamlas.co.uk

Bryn Howel Hotel: (see page 173)

Chainbridge Hotel: Disabled access
Between canal & river Dee. Dog-friendly 3-star
T:01978 860215 www.chainbridgehotel.com

Wern Isaf Farm Caravan & Camping:
½-mile from Llangollen Wharf T:01978 860632

Abbey Farm Caravan Park:
By Valle Crucis Abbey ruins T:01978 861297
www.abbeyfarmcaravans.co.uk

Dock House:
In basin, 50 yards from Pontcysyllte Aqueduct
T:0117 3041122 www.anglowelsh.co.uk

Borrows Rest B&B:
By Pontcysyllte Aqueduct T:01978 822933
www.borrows-rest-canalside.wales.info

Bryn Meirion B&B:
Canalside. 4-star T:01978 861911
www.users.globalnet.co.uk/~jhurle

Eat & drink

Tea Room & Gift shop:
Llangollen Wharf T:01978 860702

Corn Mill:
By river Dee below canal T:01978 869555

Sun Trevor:
Overlooking canal at bridge 41
T:01978 860651 www.suntrevor.co.uk

Bude

Lobster pots on the canal bank, the spray of Atlantic salt rolling in the air and gulls squawking overhead: the Bude Canal tells a different story to other canals. It's the canal on the beach, spilling out from enormous lock gates onto the golden Cornish sands of Summerleaze Beach. Once cutting 35½ miles inland, only the first 2 miles from the beach remain intact. Despite its size Bude Canal still manages to magnificently compost Cornwall's wild waterways heritage with today's cool seaside abandon of Cornish ice creams and sand castles. The canal was originally opened in 1823 to carry mainly sand, limestone, coal and farm manures but after the railways reached Bude in 1898, the canal fell into disuse, letting nature reclaim most of its route. The sea locks were restored in 2000 and regeneration goes on to bring original features back to life without disturbing local wildlife and nature. The 2-mile stretch from Bude to Helebridge is being made fully navigable for boats, but mainly with paddles and oars in mind rather than the narrowboats you see on other canals.

On the water

You can enjoy messing about on the water, rowing lazily until sunset. Or go canoeing or kayaking in the safety of gentle canal waters and, if you're not a beginner, when you reach the canal end you can carry on into the sea. Rowing boats and pedalos are available for hire by the hour from the wharf, near the sea lock. It is possible to continue along the canal a short way, but be careful as you go under the road bridge. When the original Falcon Bridge was replaced with a modern road bridge, it was lowered and left barely any head room.

The sea lock

Bude Canal's sea lock is one of only two in the UK opening directly to the sea and is a Scheduled Ancient Monument. It was built to allow sea vessels into the wharf for trading and still operates today. Set in a huge breakwater to protect and enhance the wharf area, it has had to be repaired many times, the most recent being in 2008 when a storm wrenched one of the gates off its hinges!

Tub boats

Bude was the first canal in the UK, second in the world, to use water-powered tub boats and first in the world to use tub boats with permanent iron wheels. The canal had six inclined planes, the most on any one canal, which were a means of transferring boats up a hill without building a lock. The boats were pulled up out of the water on rails, with water wheels or giant buckets of water driving the chains to raise them to the next level where they were then re-floated to continue on their way.

Further info:
You can see an example of a tub boat in the museum (see following page).

Tides

Tides change the huge flat expanse of Summerleaze Beach. At low tide, boats are left stranded and at high tide, it's easier to see how the canal connects with the sea.

Details:
Find out online tidal information with low and high tide times from Admiralty Easy Tide http://easytide.ukho.gov.uk

On the towpath

The towpath has recently been laid with a good surface for easy walking. It's up to you whether to enjoy a gentle stroll 'there and back' along the canal's two restored miles or loop off the beaten track to cliff tops following the coastal path home. For cyclists, Sustrans' signposts of the West Country Way, National Cycle Network route 3, tempt you to go further.

Details:
Walk leaflets and further information are available from Bude Tourist Information Centre. For information about Sustrans and the National Cycle Network, see page 69.

Bude & Stratton Town Museum

Housed in the former canal blacksmith's shop, the museum explores the history of Bude Canal. The collection includes the only known example of a Bude Canal tub boat, complete with wheels.

Details:
Bude & Stratton Town Museum T:01288 353576 Open April to September.

Further info:
Tourist Information Centre: Bude T:01288 354240 www.visitbude.info
Bude Canal and Harbour Society: T:01288 352808 www.bude-canal.co.uk
More info on Bude Canal and other canals - www.waterscape.com

And more...

Sleep

Breakwater House B&B: (see page 181)
Canalside near sea lock

Court Farm Holidays: 4-star Dog-friendly
Marhamchurch. Short walk from end of canal
T:01288 361494 www.courtfarm-holidays.co.uk

Harbour Loft:
Overlooking Summerleaze Beach & sea lock
T:01288 352082 www.harbourloft.co.uk

Mallards, The Old Laundry: Dog-friendly
Canalside with private jetty & rowing boat
T:01297 560033/822 www.mallards-bude.co.uk

Primrose Cottage:
Canalside near sea lock
T:01288 354004/356791 4-star Dog-friendly
www.primrosecottagebude.co.uk

Seascape:
Canalside overlooking beach T:01288 356195
www.atlanticsaltaireholidays.co.uk

Stapletons, The Old Laundry:
Canalside with private jetty & boat
T:07743 820293 www.theoldlaundrybude.co.uk

Brendon Arms: (Guest rooms)
By Falcon Bridge. Also contact them for
Captain's Cottage & Lifeboat House Apts
T:01288 354542 www.brendonarms.co.uk

Eat & drink

Castle Restaurant & Tearoom: T:01288 350543
In Castle Heritage Centre at the wharf
www.thecastlerestaurantbude.co.uk

The Brasserie: (see page 79)

Falcon Hotel & Inn: (see page 173)

Hebden Bridge

An unassuming canal town scrambles the romantic landscape of moors, crags and valleys hugging its heritage of old cotton and woollen mills with scatterings of statuesque chimneys looming in iconic loneliness. The Rochdale Canal, affectionately known as the 'Everest of Britain's canals', was the first trans-Pennine route and its canal town of Hebden Bridge thrived on the Industrial Revolution, famously producing corduroy and moleskin. A dormant industrial past adds bagfuls of charm to the northern skyline today and Hebden Bridge has matured into a deliciously nonconformist hive. Tucked along the waterside the tiny town is stuffed with Pennine charisma and you'll find it bubbling with brown rice, rainbow hats, an inordinate ratio of well-mannered waggy dogs and happy free-range kids. It's a town of walkers, cyclists and boaters too, all savouring the reaches of Calderdale's great outdoors. The eco-ethics of Hebden Bridge's intimate community unmistakably permeate the gentle stream of visitors.

HEBDEN BRIDGE

VISITOR & CANAL CENTRE

· VISITOR INFORMATION & · ACCOMMODATION BOOKING

Eco shopping

When you first arrive the town sign enlightens you in advance, telling you it's the Pennine Centre. A town of quaint little shops. And that's what you get. A shop browser's paradise without even a whiff downwind of a chain store. You can buy anything from fancy striped bows of pasta to handmade wind chimes. Hebden Bridge was one of the first towns in Britain to encourage the use of alternatives to plastic bags, so be happy to bring your rucksacks. The hub of shops, cafés and pubs centres around the bridge itself, which dates back to 1477 in its original wooden structure before the stone bridge you see today replaced it around 30 years later. The town has spread onto the canal since the 1970s with a colourful residential community of permanently moored narrowboats. It all adds up to the small local ethos giving Hebden Bridge its distinctive alternative energy and enviable egalitarian culture. Its hempy image may invite scorn from doubters, but don't be fooled by critics, this place is too far north for pretentious tokenistic recycled wrappings. It's the real thing in Hebden Bridge, right through to its wholesome core.

Further info:
The 'bag ladies' of Hebden Bridge started the campaign to ban the use of plastic bags in 2007 and, at the time, Hebden was the largest town in Europe to do so.

Heptonstall

It's mandatory to climb the steep hill from Hebden Bridge to experience this quintessential place where time has stood still. Like many Yorkshire villages, Heptonstall once thrived as a centre for handloom weaving and its cobblestoned history will fill your hill-weary lungs as you sightsee the weavers' cottages around the aptly named Weavers' Square, the 16th-century Cloth Hall and Heptonstall Museum. In the churchyard you'll find the gravestone of Sylvia Plath, wife of the poet laureate Ted Hughes who was born in nearby Mytholmroyd.

Canalside pub

There's no shortage of cosy pubs in Hebden Bridge but for the canalside pub experience, drop in at the Stubbing Wharf. Typically for Hebden Bridge you won't find frills or candelabras, just a genuinely warm non-clichéd northern welcome with the canny Hebden mix of people (locals, walkers, cyclists, boaters and the occasional guide writer!) The food is big. Huge. And the town's ethics ensure it's locally sourced whenever possible. Kids don't get inferior plates of commercially shaped e-numbers, just smaller portions of food good enough for grown-ups but half the price.

Details:
The Stubbing Wharf T:0870 0348443 www.stubbingwharf.com Dogs welcome
Ask for a latte and you'll get it, but try the real ale to get the taste buds really going. We tried Golden Pippin from Skipton Brewery - delicious! Regular short boat trips run from just outside the pub.

Little Valley Brewery

The local brewery sits high above Cragg Valley and pumps out beer as pure as Hebden Bridge itself. With the heady approval of CAMRA, the Soil Association and the Vegan Society, it's definitely good ethical drinking.

Details:
Little Valley Brewery T:01422 883888 www.littlevalleybrewery.co.uk

Organic House

When in Hebden Bridge do as Hebdenians do: go organic. The Organic House has a great atmosphere and great cakes!

Details:
Organic House T:01422 843429 www.organic-house.co.uk Organic vegetarian

Further info:
Boat hire: Bronte Boat Hire T:01706 815103 www.bronteboathire.co.uk
Walkers: www.hbwalkersaction.org.uk
Alternative Technology Centre: Hebden Bridge www.alternativetechnology.org.uk
Visitor & Canal Centre: Hebden Bridge T:01422 843831 www.enjoyengland.com
More info on Rochdale Canal and other canals - www.waterscape.com

EXTRA RESERVE TASTY
LANCASHIRE

£1.05 per 100g

SUITABLE FOR VEGETARIANS

CREAMY LANCASHIRE
Traditional creamy Lancashire from Dewlay

96p per 100g

V = Suitable for Vegetarians

BRIE

£1.19 per

VIGNOTTE

£1.36 per 100g

BOUCHE

MANCHEGO

MUND

SOMERSET BRIE
Made with the milk of Jersey cows for a
rich creamy taste

£1.15 per 100g

V = Suitable for Vegetarians

TUNKING BISHOP

£1.16 p

mooch
cafe+bar

FAIRTRADE

Guarantees
a better deal
Third World
Producers

And more...

Where to sleep

Laurel End House: (see page 181)
Overlooking the canal

Croft Mill Apartments: (see page 189)
Overlooking the canal

Melbourne Mill:
Apartment, a short walk from the canal
T:01244 356695 www.sykescottages.co.uk

White Lion Hotel:
Short walk from the canal
T:01422 842197 www.whitelionhotel.net

Dusty Miller:
Short walk from bridge 11, Mytholmroyd
T:01422 885959 Guest bedrooms

Eat &drink

Stubbing Wharf: (see page 222)
Canalside near Stubbing Upper Lock

White Lion Hotel: See above
Short walk from the canal

Mooch Café Bar:
Along the main street
T:01422 846954

Organic House: (see page 222)
Along the main street

Dusty Miller: See above
Mytholmroyd

Cross Inn:
Heptonstall T:01422 843833

White Lion:
Heptonstall T:01422 842027

Stratford-upon-Avon

A town scribed in history, pouting with Englishness as it sends Tudor charm beaming through its wide streets of tourists. The River Avon bustles with rowing boats and holiday boats. The infamous Royal Shakespeare Theatre, opened in 1932 and currently undergoing restoration, performs elegantly from the riverbank building while swans and geese lurk on the water like gangs of Capulets and Montagues. Meanwhile, in almost any weather, picnickers sprawl the river's grassy banks, some grabbing refreshments from the Baguette Barge or the floating ice cream van in the adjoining canal basin. Shakespeare's Stratford is naturally one of Britain's top tourist attractions, luring hoards of bard-seeking visitors every year but, luckily for canal goers, few of the madding crowd spot the canal quietly ambling past town, beyond the river, disappearing into the deepest greens of Warwickshire's countryside.

Stratford-upon-Avon Canal

The Stratford-upon-Avon Canal treads the heart of Shakespeare's own territory, away from the trumpeting of trinket shops. The quaint olde worlde scatterings of black and white cottages blend with the colours of British Waterways and the green smells of earth are only mildly blighted by the occasional hum of the distant motorway. You'll meet some unusual features on this canal. Mini aqueducts let you stand level with the water and peer over metal sides into the canal, as if it were held in a chunky bathtub with cars passing underfoot. Then there are curiously shaped barrel-roofed lock keepers' cottages. On the towpath at the edge of town you might stumble upon the 21st-century ramblings of rebel bards come aerosol graffiti vandals. Thankfully such messy interruption is short-lived and soon forgiven as the canal quietly leads you into a more tranquil haven.
Like most canals the Stratford has at times faced struggles for its survival. In 1959 passionate protests riled against the canal's closure and gutsy restoration work from volunteers led to this section of the canal being reopened in 1964. Scattered along the canal you'll spot plaques commemorating its reopening that read, "we were not experts therefore we did not know what could not be done".

Barrel-roofed cottages

The mysteriously barrel-roofed lock cottages that line the water are a real feature of this canal. The truth behind the quirk is purely practical: engineers building the Stratford-upon-Avon Canal knew more about building bridges than houses so when they had to build lock cottages for the lengthsmen, it resulted in cottages with curious barrel-shaped roofs. Look out for the barrel-roofed garden shed one householder has amusingly erected on their canalside lawn.

Further info:
See page 185 for details of a barrel-roofed cottage available for holiday lets.

Split bridges

Specially designed bridges were built in two sections with a gap down the centre allowing a rope to slip through. When boats were pulled along by horses, the towrope would have tugged straight through these bridges, saving time (which was money) to the working crews.

Aqueducts

The Stratford-upon-Avon Canal has three unusual aqueducts: Yarningale, Wootton Wawen and Edstone (also known as Bearley). Towpaths are usually higher than a canal's water level; however, on these aqueducts, the towpath is level with the base of the canal trough so, as you walk across, the water is almost level with your shoulders rather than your feet.

Royal Shakespeare Company (RSC)

The RSC are probably the most famous theatre company in the world and aim to keep modern audiences in touch with Shakespeare.

Details:
Stratford-upon-Avon. T:01789 403444 www.rsc.org.uk
The theatre is currently undergoing a transformation, which is due to be completed by 2010. Until then, performances are continuing at the Courtyard Theatre and other venues around Stratford.

Shakespeare Birthplace Trust

Working to preserve and maintain properties, books, manuscripts and other records connected with, or relating to, Shakespeare. They also promote appreciation and study of his plays and works across the world.

Details:
Stratford-upon-Avon. Tel: 01789 204016 www.shakespeare.org.uk

Further info:
Boat hire: Anglo Welsh Waterway Holidays, Wootton Wawen T:0117 3041122 www.anglo-welsh.co.uk
Tourist Information Centre: Stratford-upon-Avon T:0870 1607930 www.shakespeare-country.co.uk
Holy Trinity Church: Shakespeare is buried here. T:01789 266316 www.stratford-upon-avon.org
More info on Stratford-upon-Avon Canal and other canals - www.waterscape.com

THE NATIONAL TRUST
STRATFORD ON AVON CANAL

THE ERECTION OF THIS BRIDGE,
CONSTRUCTED BY MEN FROM
H.M. PRISON
WORMWOOD SCRUBS
AND H.M. PRISON
BIRMINGHAM
COMPLETED THE RESTORATION
TO NAVIGATION OF THE CANAL
BY VOLUNTEERS, SERVICEMEN
AND PRISONERS
1961-4

THE CANAL
WAS RE-OPENED BY
H.M. QUEEN ELIZABETH
THE QUEEN MOTHER
ON
SATURDAY 11TH JULY 1964

Fleur de Lys

KINGS
NORTON
22
MILES

SONAC

And more...

Where to sleep
Acanthus Cottage & Apple Loft:
Wilmcote. Short walk from canal. 4-star
T:01789 205889 www.peartreecot.co.uk

1 Bancroft Place:
Canalside studio apartment T:01295 690335
www.selfcatering-directory.co.uk

4 Bancroft Place:
Studio apartment overlooking the canal. 3-star
T:01920 871849 www.4bancroftplace.com

Lengthsman's Cottage: (see page 185)
Canalside by Lock 31 T:01628 825925

Mary Arden Inn:
Opposite the home of Shakespeare's mother
T:01789 267030 www.mary-arden.co.uk

Eat & drink
Pen & Parchment:
Near the Basin T:01789 297697

Baguette Barge & Avon Ices: (see page 79)
Stratford-upon-Avon T:07963 956720

Boot Inn:
Near Lock 14, Lapworth.
T:01564 782464 www.bootinnlapworth.co.uk

The Fleur de Lys:
Canalside near Lock 31 T:01564 782431
www.fleurdelys-lowsonford.com

Navigation Inn:
Canalside by Wootton Wawen Aqueduct
T:01564 792676 www.the-navigationinn.co.uk

Our top 10 canals

Reducing our list of favourite canals to just ten was always going to be impossible. Every canal is different and we love them all for different reasons. Canals can be wide or narrow, busy with or barren of leisure boats, meaty with engineering features or quietly flat. Most are conventionally beautiful in the rural sense and others ask to be loved for other reasons. The practicalities of its original purpose dictates that the water road belongs, in parts, to territories such as the so-called Dark Satanic Mills, the Black Country and the slums of Victorian urbanites. Don't be put off by preconceptions though, industry can be aesthetically stunning with a view from the water. Britain's waterways world, like any other tourist destination around the globe, has pockets of grimy truths the brochures prefer to ignore and inevitably canals will occasionally straggle through despicable zones of city neglect. Some canals like the Leeds & Liverpool promise you the very best and worst of times. Around Skipton, it's spectacular amidst Pennine panache yet Lancashire's worst hooligan towns can blot the canal beyond. The Rochdale Canal is similarly contradictory, unbeatable in parts and teetering on foul in others. To make our task easier, our top ten canals are those we think offer the best all-round experience along the entire canal.

Crinan Canal

Nothing compares to this! A short canal tucked away in tartan Highlands. The wild west coast of Scotland calls this their short cut; and they are talking about seafaring vessels not narrowboats. Essential accessories are woollies and walking boots. Truly stunning.

Details: **Crinan to Ardrishaig. 9 miles**

Caledonian Canal

Epic, breathtaking and all superlatives; words cannot adequately describe this coast-to-coast waterway piping across the Scottish Highlands, swelling from canal into lochs, in the company of a cheeky monster.

Details: **Fort William to Inverness. 60 miles**

Llangollen Canal

The canal that's got everything. From Cheshire's green fields to the mountains of Wales it's never less than idyllic, and it's all wrapped up in the drama of the incredible Pontcysyllte Aqueduct (see page 243).

Details: **Hurleston Junction to Llantysilio (only navigable to Llangollen). 46 miles**

Monmouthshire & Brecon Canal

The peaceful canal. Rambling high in the Brecon Breacons, it's a heady cocktail of water and views and, because it's landlocked from the main cruising networks, this canal is ultra calm.

Details: **Cwmbran to Brecon. 35 miles**

Macclesfield Canal

Skidaddling from the Midlands into Cheshire's scenery then bursting onto the brink of the Pennines, this canal is deliciously picturesque. There's plenty to see along the way including Little Morton Hall, one of Britain's best timbered buildings from the 1500s. Aesthetically, it features distinctive roving bridges with swirling brickwork (once enabling boat horses to swap sides on the towpath without uncoupling from their narrowboats).

Details: **Hardings Wood Junction to Marple. 26¾ miles**

Kennet & Avon Canal

From the cultured beat of Bristol with its harbour life to a meeting with the Thames at Reading, it's a waterway cutting through some of England's most green and pleasant lands. Winds through Wiltshire's mystical villages and Bath's Georgian crescents with their nuances of Jane Austen.

Details: Bristol to Reading. 100 miles. Caen Hill Flight - one of the 7 Wonders (see page 243)

Oxford Canal

Full of Oxford grace, this canal tours Warwickshire's farmlands passing Napton with its hilltop windmill and travelling through idyllic villages with irresistible real ale pubs. One highlight of the canal is the quintessentially English village of Cropredy - adored by boaters, frequented by tourists and infused with folkieness.

Details: Oxford to Hawkesbury Junction. 77 miles

Peak Forest Canal

Never spoiling your fun by getting too close to Manchester, the canal is a raw escape with views over the Goyt valley and crescendos over the delights of the Peak District.

Details: Whaley Bridge to Dukinfield Junction. 15 miles

Staffordshire & Worcestershire Canal

Dangerously close to the urban masses of the Midlands but miraculously rural. Fiery red sandstone rocks overhang the water in the prettiest section from Kinver to Wolverley, rivalling any canal for beauty. The river awaits at Stourport, the only town built especially for the canals.

Details: Great Haywood to Stourport-on-Severn. 46 miles

Stratford-upon-Avon Canal

Secretly away from Stratford-upon-Avon's tourists, this is an utterly English inland waterway. Black and white cottages, Shakespearian heritage distractions and the romance of the River Avon.

Details: King's Norton Junction to Stratford. 25½ miles

The 7 wonders of the Waterways

Robert Aickman, founder of the Inland Waterways' Association, drew up a list over fifty years ago of the most amazing canal engineering feats:

Pontcysyllte Aqueduct

See narrowboats fly through the sky on the UK's highest aqueduct, 127ft above the Dee
Location: Trevor Basin. Llangollen Canal OS SJ270420 (see also page 203)
Further info: Nominated for World Heritage Site status. Decision to be announced in 2009.

Standedge Tunnel

3¼ miles long, a tunnel through the Pennines, as if they weren't in the way at all
Details: Standedge Tunnel & Visitor Centre T:01484 844298 www.standedge.co.uk
Location: Marsden. Huddersfield Narrow Canal OS SE040120
Further info: Open April to October. Visitor Centre with cafe, guided & through boat trips

Anderton Boat Lift

The 'cathedral' of the canals carries boats from the Trent & Mersey Canal to the Weaver
Details: Anderton Boat Lift T:01606 786777 www.andertonboatlift.co.uk
Location: Anderton, Northwich. Trent & Mersey Canal, Weaver Navigation OS SJ647753
Further info: Visitor Centre open from February, boat lift and river trips March to October

Barton Swing Aqueduct

A canal full of water amazingly swings out of the way for ships on the canal below
Details: Barton Swing Aqueduct carries the Bridgewater Canal over the Manchester Ship Canal
Location: Barton upon Irwell. Bridgewater Canal OS SJ767976
Further info: Operates all year except for maintenance. Road bridge also swings open.

Bingley 5 Rise

Unique 5-lock staircase to heaven carries the canal up 60 feet above the woollen mills of Bingley
Details: Bingley Five Rise. Boat passage through flight Mon-Fri needs to be booked T:0113 2816860
Location: Bingley. Leeds & Liverpool Canal OS SE107399

Burnley Embankment

The 'straight mile' carries the canal over the rooftops of Burnley, near the Weavers' Triangle
Details: Burnley Embankment. Almost a mile long and up to 60ft high in places
Location: Burnley. Leeds & Liverpool Canal OS SD844325

Caen Hill Flight

16 wide locks pounded closely together take boats miraculously up and down the hill
Details: Caen Hill Flight, the highlight of 29 locks in the 2¼ miles leading to Devizes
Location: Devizes. Kennet & Avon Canal OS ST983614

Not in the original list, a new 8th wonder - The Falkirk Wheel

An incredible engineering marvel, the world's first & only rotating boat lift, opened in 2002
Details: Falkirk Wheel. 08700 500208 www.thefalkirkwheel.co.uk
Location: Falkirk. Lifts boats 115ft between the Union and Forth & Clyde Canals OS NS852801

NATIONAL   WATE·RWAYS   MUSEUM

LLANTHONY WAREHOUSE

YOUR LOCAL CANAL OR RIVER

It's an
open-air gym

Yours to enjoy. Anyone.

Find your nearest canal or river at waterscape.com

YOUR LOCAL CANAL OR RIVER

It's a
relaxation class

Yours to enjoy. Anyone.

Find your nearest canal or river at waterscape.com

Waterways Who's Who

The great engineers:

James Brindley (1716-1772)
Pioneering genius responsible for the first canals and for developing the concept of canal networks

John Rennie (1761-1821)
Famous for bridges and canal engineering, such as Dundas Aqueduct on the Kennet & Avon Canal

Thomas Telford (1757-1834)
Prolific engineer responsible for marvels such as Pontcysyllte Aqueduct & second Harecastle Tunnel

The great entrepreneurs:

Josiah Wedgwood (1730-1795)
The Potteries drove canal developers with support, especially for the Trent & Mersey Canal

John Cadbury (1801-1889)
One of many Quaker social reformers and businessmen who supported the canals. Cocoa beans were carried by waterway from Bristol docks to Birmingham to the famous Cadbury's chocolate factories.

Sir Titus Salt (1803-1876)
Wool baron who created Saltaire village (now a World Heritage Site) for his mill workers on the Leeds & Liv Canal. Similar to Bournville built by John Cadbury's son for workers in Birmingham, both had a distinct absence of pubs due to Quaker influence until a bar 'Don't Tell Titus' opened at Saltaire in 2007.

And today…

British Waterways (BW)
Governing body responsible for 2,200 miles of Britain's canals and rivers. www.british-waterways.co.uk

Waterscape
BW's official guide to canals, rivers and lakes. www.waterscape.com

Inland Waterways' Association (IWA)
Founded by Thomas Rolt and Robert Aickman in 1946. Rolt fought ceaselessly to keep the waterways open for his narrowboat Cressy and for future generations of boaters. www.waterways.org.uk

Waterways Trust
National charity promoting greater public enjoyment of inland waterways. www.thewaterwaystrust.co.uk

Waterway Recovery Group (WRG)
Voluntary organisation, running work camps to help restore derelict canals. www.wrg.org.uk

National Waterways Museums
One museum in three locations. Largest collection of historic boats in the world, interactive displays and Waterways Archive preserving artefacts of canal history back to the 1700s. www.nwm.org.uk

The Canal Trusts and Societies
The bodies tackling restoration and management of the inland waterways. Most canals have an active Trust or Society with regular events, meetings, talks and fundraising.
Why not join your local canal society?

Useful info

Tourist Boards

Enjoy England
www.enjoyengland.com
Visit Scotland
www.visitscotland.com
Visit Wales
www.visitwales.com

Travel

Buses: Traveline
T:0871 2002233 www.traveline.org.uk
Trains: National Rail Enquiries
T:08457 484950 www.nationalrail.co.uk

Waterways' magazines/newspapers

Canals & Rivers
www.canalsandrivers.co.uk
Canal Boat
www.canalboat.co.uk
Towpath Talk
www.towpathtalk.co.uk
Waterways World
www.waterwaysworld.com

Boating & outdoors

Royal Yachting Association (RYA)
Represents the interests of anyone who boats
for pleasure
www.rya.org.uk
The Green Blue
Advice on environmentally conscious boating
www.thegreenblue.org.uk
Direct Enquiries
National disabled access register
www.directenquiries.com
Ramblers' Association
Walking information and canal walks
www.ramblers.org.uk

Glossary

Aqueduct: structure carrying a canal over a road, railway or river

Arm: short stretch of canal branching off from the main canal

Barge: cargo-carrying boat which is 16ft wide or more

Beam: width of a boat

Bow: front of a boat

Broad canal: canal over 7ft 6in wide

BW: British Waterways (see page 245)

Butty: unpowered boat towed by another boat with an engine

Canalia: gifts and crafts related to canals

Cratch: triangular structure at bow of boat

Cruiser: pleasure boat usually made of wood or fibreglass

Cruiser stern: extended external space at rear end of a narrowboat

Cut: slang for canal

Dolly: post used to tie mooring ropes round

Fender: externally hung bumpers, usually made of rope, to protect hull of boat

Flight: series of locks closely pounded together

Gongoozler: Boaters' lingo describing onlookers

Gunwales: (pronounced gunnels) ridge along sides of narrowboat

IWA: Inland Waterways' Association (see page 245)

Junction: where two or more canals meet

Legging: lying on top of boat and using legs on walls to push boat through tunnel

Lock: a water-holding chamber with gates and paddles to lift boats up and down hills

Milepost: short posts informing boatmen about distances travelled

Narrowboat: canal boats which are no wider than 7ft

Narrow canal: canals built for boats up to 70ft long and 7ft wide

Navvies: nickname for the navigators who dug the canals

Port: left side of boat when facing the bow

Pound: stretch of level water between locks, whether a few feet or a few miles

Roses and Castles: traditional folk art (see page 105)

Scumble: painting technique simulating the appearance of wood grain

Silt: mud that builds up at bottom of canal

Starboard: right side of the boat when facing the bow

Staircase locks: locks close together without pounds between

Stern: the rear of a boat

Tiller: steering wheel of a boat, shaped like a pole

Towpath: path alongside canal built for working horses pulling boats

Tug: boat that pulls another boat

Tupperware: humorously irreverent name narrowboaters give fibreglass boats

Waterways Trust: charitable body (see page 245)

Wide beam narrowboat: boat that looks like a narrowboat but is wider than 7ft 6in

Windlass: hand tool used to wind lock paddles up and down

How this book happened

It's one of those dreams - to dip out from the norm, give up the humdrum rush of everyday and escape to the freedom of living on the water in a narrowboat. We did it, and took our four cats with us.

We ditched the house, car, TV and washing machine for a simple eco life on the water. We built the interior of our narrowboat-home out of reclaimed wood and launched a new off-grid lifestyle travelling Britain's inland waterways.

Living on a narrowboat means slowing down to canal time and enjoying the basic things in life. Gathering logs for the stove, boiling a kettle from rationed water, starting the day at first light and ending it watching the night's stars. It's an outdoor lifestyle where most of the good things are free and 'make do and mend' isn't drudgery. Somehow priorities change.

We explored as far as our boat could take us and then, determined to stay waterways nomads, we decided to swap our boat for boots to walk all the canals of Britain, from Cornwall to Scotland.

This special place is one of Britain's best treasures. We've discovered how surprising canals can be and launched Coolcanals Guides to share some of our discoveries.

We hope from our guides you'll explore something different from your norm, find your own escape.

Photo Index: places

Index